The Picture Book
of *Vaseline Glass*

Sue C. Davis

Photographed
by
Bill McFarling

Schiffer Publishing Ltd

4880 Lower Valley Road, Atglen, PA 19310 USA

Dedication

I would like to dedicate this book to my nephew, Ben Curtis, who at the age of twelve recognizes and appreciates the beauty and value of this beautiful glass, and has become an avid collector. His comments to me when he was four years old were, "Aunt Susan, can we turn on those lights that glow?" When we did, he said, "Now, this is just gorgeous!"

Designed by "Sue"
Type set in Dutch 801 ItHd BT/ Goudy OlStBt

ISBN: 0-7643-0830-0
Printed in China
1 2 3 4

Published by Schiffer Publishing Ltd.
4880 Lower Valley Road
Atglen, PA 19310
Phone: (610) 593-1777; Fax: (610) 593-2002
E-mail: Schifferbk@aol.com
Please visit our web site catalog at **www.schifferbooks.com**

This book may be purchased from the publisher.
Include $3.95 for shipping.
Please try your bookstore first.
We are interested in hearing from authors
with book ideas on related subjects.
You may write for a free catalog.

In Europe, Schiffer books are distributed by
Bushwood Books
6 Marksbury Rd.
Kew Gardens
Surrey TW9 4JF England
Phone: 44 (0)181 392-8585; Fax: 44 (0)181 392-9876
E-mail: Bushwd@aol.com

Contents

Acknowledgments

I would like to acknowledge my family and many friends as well as the collectors and dealers who encouraged me to publish this book. A special thanks goes to Bill McFarling for his excellent photography; to Larry and Lois Smith, Pete and Laura Kelm Buck, and Ben Curtis for sharing their Vaseline Glass collections; to Melanie Schonier for sharing selections from her extensive inventory; to Lena Lou Staton for sharing her experience and her assistance with pricing; and to Schiffer Publishing for recognizing the value of a book of this type and publishing it.

Chapter 1.
An Introduction to Vaseline Glass

Welcome to *The Picture Book of Vaseline Glass*. This book is offered with two main objectives in mind, knowledge and pleasure. I am sure there are many of you, like me, who at times just enjoy relaxing and looking at pretty pictures of glass. I am equally sure there are times when you want and need information on glass. Therefore, this book, with its more than 450 photographs and as much information as I could find on each of the 675 different pieces of glass shown, is presented in hopes that it will provide the novice and seasoned glass collector alike with some knowledge and a lot of pleasure. Enjoy!

The Informed Glass Buyer

There is little doubt that many dealers of antiques and collectibles are thoroughly familiar with the items they sell. Still, in today's market, there are dealers who become involved solely because of the potential to make money in the buying and selling of old things. One can easily see this trend by observing the large number of flea markets, antiques malls, and collectibles malls where there are rows after rows of booths exhibiting various pieces ranging from recent to ancient vintage.

Collectors can observe the rise in antiques and collectibles shows that feature similar kinds of items. Sellers may or may not be interested in the specific names, patterns, ages, or locations where the items they sell were made. This is not a critique of the current state of the antiques and collectibles market, but is a statement about the need for the collectors of glassware, whatever the time frame, to be aware of what they are purchasing. Often questions to dealers are answered with, "I'm not sure of what this is, how old it is, or who manufactured it." Even in some of the smaller antiques and collectibles auctions that take place, usually on a weekly or monthly basis, in communities around these United States, auctioneers will readily tell buyers that "they are purchasing an item at their own risk." These auction houses usually make no claim about the authenticity of any object being offered for sale. The Latin term *caveat emptor,* "let the buyer beware," is very appropriate when purchasing antiques and collectibles.

As a result of this attitude in today's marketplace, collectors and dealers are left with the task of researching their own purchases. Books such as this one are very helpful in this process, since "a picture is worth a thousand words." I encourage collectors to observe and compare, as much as possible, the pieces of Vaseline Glass in their collections and those they find in their searches with the pieces in this book. One of my good friends in the antiques business always cautioned me when I said, "I have a piece just like that one!" He would ask, " Exactly like this one? Does yours have...?"

He was training me always to observe:

1. Pattern
2. Size
3. Color
4. Manufacturer's marks, labels, logos
5. Shape (especially the top edges)

Even though many shops and malls have signs that read, "If I break, I cry. If you break, you buy," one should always carefully examine glass for cracks, chips, dings, or other flaws, which make the piece less than mint condition. This examination process is particularly important when one is purchasing at an auction. Auction houses regularly remind buyers they buy "as is, where is." This means the auction house will not assume responsibility for any flaws in the item purchased. Many buyers will get caught up in the buying frenzy, even though they did not thoroughly examine the piece before the auction started. How many times have I seen sad faces when buyers have collected their purchases from the auction house and discovered a chip or crack? Too many to count! Glassware especially is in need of close examination because of the many possibilities for small cracks or chips that hide within the pattern.

Whether or not you are buying from a dealer in a mall, an auction house, a flea market, an estate, a garage sale, or an individual, please do not hesitate to take this book with you. Do not feel rushed to purchase Vaseline Glass because it "seems" right, or it "looks" good, or even because it is such a "bargain"! That "feeling" can quickly fade to disappointment unless you have done everything possible to protect yourself. You should always keep this book and a black light handy and use them when purchasing your next piece of Vaseline Glass. Pocket size black lights are adequate for testing fluorescence and can be purchased at lighting speciality stores. The pictures in this book are taken under black light. To assist the reader in recognizing this glass in the malls, antiques shops, and flea markets, a boot is shown below, taken under black light in the first photo and without black light in the second photo.

Boyd *High Boot*, made 10/98, 4.15"h x 4.6"l. $16-20.

Once you have purchased that special piece of Vaseline Glass, a great deal of consideration should be given to displaying the piece in your home. Several of my collector friends have adopted my display ideas for their collections. Because of its versatility, I use my Vaseline Glass in all areas of my home. The beauty and elegance of this glass can be enhanced by the liberal use of mirrors. Its appearance can be subtly changed by the use of different lighting techniques. Exposed to direct sunlight, the glass will brighten a room with its brilliant glow. I like to keep a few small pieces in my kitchen window to brighten my day. Under fluorescent light, the glass is a sparkling yellow. A combination of fluorescent and black light produces a sparkling yellow with a hint of a fluorescing glow. Black light alone gives the intense distinctive fluorescent glow of Vaseline Glass. I also use antique furniture to display my glass. With the addition of glass shelves, mirrors, and a combination of fluorescent and black lights, many different pieces of antique and modern furniture can be utilized as display cases. A few suggestions are china cabinets, pie safes, lawyer bookcases, wardrobes, old display cases used in dry goods stores, jewelry display cases, and glass enclosed stereo cabinets. Built-in, well lighted shelves of glass backed by mirrors also are a good choice for display. Another unique idea is the use of a fish aquarium equipped with fluorescent and black lights. Displaying this glass is limited only by your imagination.

My quest for the beautiful, sometimes elusive, and often expensive Vaseline Glass has taken me from coast to coast. The value of my glass cannot be measured solely from a monetary aspect. Its true value comes from the joy it brings me. When I am tired, I can turn on the black lights, sit down, relax, and enjoy just looking at the glass. It never fails to make me smile when I flip the switch on the showcase. So, I hope you will find your own quest as exciting and rewarding as I have. Happy hunting!

About the Prices

The prices in this book are not intended to set prices, which are influenced by availability and condition, and which vary from one area of the country to another, from auction to auction, and from dealer to dealer. Rather the prices in this book should be considered replacement prices and are for glass in excellent condition, even though a few pieces shown here have some imperfections.

A Brief History of Vaseline Glass

Vaseline Glass is the current name given to glass which has that yellow color of petroleum jelly. Over the years, many names have been used to describe this amazing glass. In Glickman's book entitled *Yellow-Green Vaseline!*, he states: "Before the 1950s there is no record of the name Vaseline having been applied to glass. This fact was confirmed in a conversation I had with Frank Fenton, chairman of the board of the Fenton Art Glass Co." Other names for the glass include: Uranium glass, Canary, Topaz, Yellow glass, and Lemon glass. Norman Webber, in his book *Collecting Glass*, gave it the name "pearlene type fancy glass" In the book *Nineteenth Century Glassware*, Albert Christian Revi called it "lustered pea-spotted." Whatever the name, now it is glass that is highly collectible and enjoys increasing prices with each passing year.

Vaseline glassware, during the height of its production, served many functions ranging from practical to decorative. In the 1890s, Vaseline Glass was made in complete table settings and used daily. Other useful pieces were banquet pieces, lamps, door knobs, medicinal bottles, vanity sets, decanters, drapery ties, and candlesticks. Some pieces, such as the novelties, were purely decorative. The popularity of these decorative styles reflects the growing interest by consumers, between the late 1890s and the 1940s, in decorative art glass. Much of the peak in art glass styles occurred between the 1920s and the 1940s, and coincident with each rise in consumer interest was the number of companies producing glass and the explosion of the pressed-glass industry around the world. Today the production of Vaseline Glass is limited to novelties and ornamental pieces.

How Vaseline Glass Is Made

Vaseline Glass, like other glassware, as described on page 211 in the book *Glass* published by Intercon Arts, basically involves a "homogeneous mixture of inorganic compounds which upon cooling, form a random molecular structure rather than a crystalline one. It is in effect a super cooled liquid. The transparency of glass is due to the fact that there are no internal surfaces of a size approaching the wave length of visible light. All glass contains silica from sand, soda, potash, and lime in varying proportions, depending upon the type of glass. There are four basic types of glass—flint glass, leaded glass or crystal, potash glass, and soda glass." Flint glass is colorless. It contains lead and potash. Lead glass is brilliant. It must contain at least 5 percent lead. Glass with 24 percent lead is considered to be crystal. Potash glass is hard glass. It contains potassium carbonate. Soda glass is generally light in weight and thin. It contains sodium carbonate.

The secret to getting the different colors in glass involves mixing the appropriate amount of each ingredient and firing the mixture at the correct temperature. Early on, glassmakers noted that by adding a small amount of uranium oxide to their formula, they could produce a brilliant yellow-colored glass. The distinguishing feature of this yellow glass is that it will fluoresce when exposed to ultra-violet light (black light). All Vaseline Glass will fluoresce when held to an ultraviolet light, but most yellow glass is not Vaseline Glass and will not glow. There are two other types of glass that will glow when exposed to black light. They are custard glass, which is a light yellow milky color, and a clear green-colored glass that was produced during the late 1920s and early 1930s. Some dealers and collectors mistakenly call the clear green glass Vaseline Glass because it will glow when exposed to black light.

On page 34 of Neila and Tom Bredehoft's book *Hobbs, Brockunier and Co., Glass*, the following formula is given for canary glass (Vaseline Glass) with the units of measure being presumably in pounds: dry sand-2000; nitrate soda-20; soda ash-912; lime-100; arsenic-4; uranium-10.

Vaseline Glass Manufacturers

The manufacturers of Vaseline Glass are numerous, and whether or not a particular manufacturer made it depends on which history of glassware you read. While small amounts of Vaseline Glass that are believed to be centuries old have been located, most glassware historians believe that the current process for producing Vaseline Glass began in the mid-1800s, but was not perfected until the 1890s.

The list of older companies that produced Vaseline Glass reads like the Who's Who in the glassware manufacturing business. They include:

Adams and Company; Alexander J. Beatty and Sons; American Glass; Philip Arogast; Belmont Glass; Boston and Sandwich Glass; Brockunier; John Bryce and Co.; Cambridge; Challinor, Taylor and Co.; Consolidated Lamp Co.; George Davidson and Co.; Doyle and Co.; George Duncan and Sons; Dugan; Fenton Art Glass; Fostoria; Gillinder and Sons; Heisey; Hobbs Glass Company; Imperial; King and Co.; Libbey; Millersburg Glass; National Glass; Nickel-Plate Glass; Northwood; Pairpoint; U.S. Glass; Westmoreland, and West Virginia Glass, among others. Some of the newer companies are Boyd Art Glass; Degenhart; Gibson; Mosser; Summit; Viking; Wheaton, and L. G. Wright.

As with many other products that were produced in the United States between 1880 and 1920, manufacturers were appealing to rapidly changing tastes within the buying public. Witness the dramatic change in furniture tastes—from the dark colors of the Victorian Era, to the appeal of Oak during the Golden Oak Period, to the stark simplicity of the Mission Styles, to the flowery styles of the Art Deco Period. Taste in glassware followed similar trends. One company might produce a style of Vaseline Glass that would be rapidly absorbed by the buying public, only to have second issues of the same design end up in stock piles on company warehouse shelves.

By the early 1900s the interest in Vaseline Glass had waned. A few companies attempted to revitalize the interest during the Art Deco Period with small success.

Vaseline Glass Patterns

Vaseline Glass has been made in many different patterns and shapes. The Daisy and Button pattern is the most common, and almost all of the glass companies produced this pattern. Following here are some of the patterns and shapes found in this book: Alaska, Argonaut Shell, Bag Ware, Barbells, Basketweave, Beaumont's Columbia, Button Panels, Cactus, Clio, Clover, Coinspot, Corn Vase, Daisy and Button, Daisy and Button with Crossbar, Daisy and Button with "V" Ornament, Daisy and Button with Thumbprint, (Paneled) Daisy and Button, Daisy and Fern, Dew Drop, Diamond Quilted, Diamond Spearhead, Dolphin, External Ribs, Fluted Scrolls, Heirloom, Hobnail, Holly Clear, Inverted Thumbprint, Inverted Fan and Feather, Iris With Meander, Lady Chippendale, Lattice and Daisy, Lattice and Thumbprint, Leaf Mold, Lorna, Maple Leaf, Medallion, Moon and Stars, Northwood Block, Old Man Winter, Opal Open or Beaded Panels, Over-All Hob, Panel Grape, Pearls and Scales, Petticoats, Peacock Feather and Thistle, Plain Jane, Princess Diana, Pump and Trough, Queen's Crown, Question Mark, Quilted Pillow Sham, Reverse Swirl, Ribbed Spiral, Richelieu, Rose Sprig, Sanibel, Single Lily Spool, Spanish Lace, Strawberry and Currant, Swag With Brackets, Thousand Eye, Three Panel, Twig, War of Roses, William and Mary, Wreath and Shell, Wreathed Cherry.

I expended a great deal of time and effort identifying these various patterns. However, I was unable to identify all the pieces. If a reader might assist with identification, it would be appreciated. Write to me in care of Schiffer Publishing, Ltd.

Reproductions

Vaseline Glass is no exception when it comes to having reproductions on the market. However, because of its scarcity, all Vaseline Glass is collectible; the difference is in the cost. Following the initial surge of interest in Vaseline Glass and other colored glassware between 1890 and 1930, many manufacturers of glassware began to reproduce some of the more popular pieces. The manufacture of glass was becoming easier and less costly than in the years prior to the 1930s. Many manufacturers decided to "cash in" on the interest in art glass. When old glass companies closed, new glass companies would purchase their molds. Sometimes the original mold was used for the reproduction. Other times, slight variations would be made in the mold. There was a surge in the reproduction of Vaseline Glass in the late 1950s to mid-1970s, and presently in the 1990s. It would serve the buyer well to study the different patterns and shapes of Vaseline Glass found in this book. Often sellers themselves do not know the difference between the original design and a reproduction, but the difference in price can be substantial. Be careful to consider shape and pattern along with studying a picture of original glass, so that an expensive error may be avoided.

A simple glance at a picture without also examining the shape and pattern, can sometimes be costly.

The following abbreviations are used in the captions that follow:

b–base
d–diameter
ea–each
h–height
l–length
nos–not original stopper
pr–pair
sq–square
TP–toothpick
w–width

Chapter II.
The Mid-1800s to the Early 1900s

Peacock plate by Sandwich Glass. This plate is an example of the *Lacy* glass design made from 1829-1840s. According to McKearin in *American Glass*, page 357 this *Peacock Feather and Thistle* pattern is found only in 8" plates and is rare in canary. 8"d. $275-300. *Courtesy of Laura Kelm and Pete Buck.*

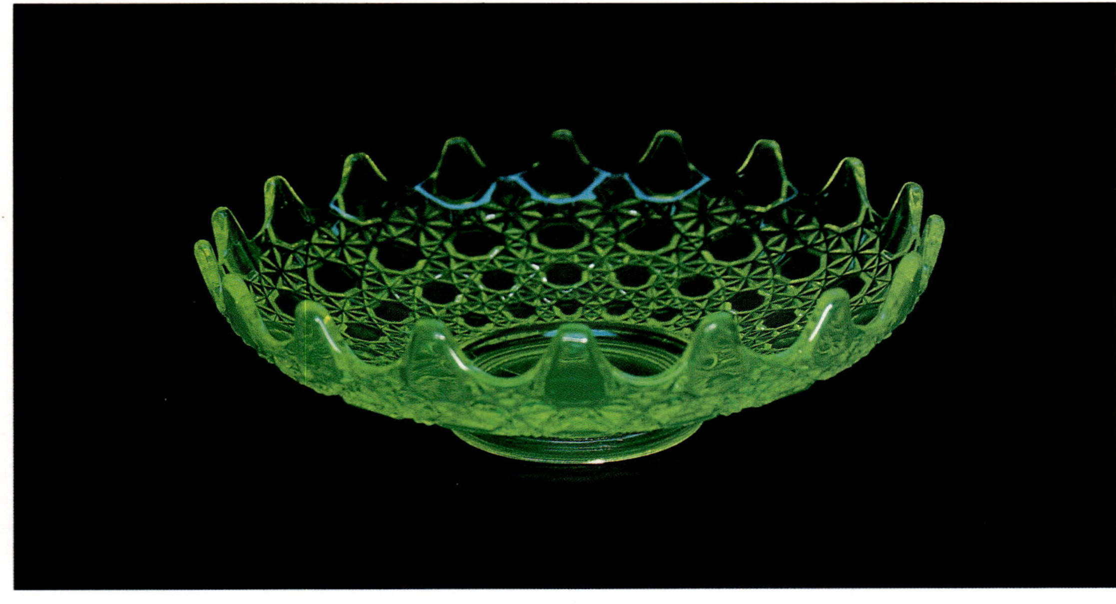

Daisy and Button fruit bowl made by U. S. Glass, c. 1890s. This large fruit bowl measures 3.5"h x 11.25"d and has a deeply scalloped rim. $300-350.

Bag Ware orange bowl made by Duncan and Sons, c. 1890-1892. According to Heacock this pattern was made with and without panels, 6.25"h x 7.75"d. $250-300.

Triangle master berry set by U. S. Glass, c. 1890s. This *Daisy and Button* master berry bowl is 3"h x 8"d. $250-300. The sauce dishes are 1"h x 4.5"d. $75-85 ea.

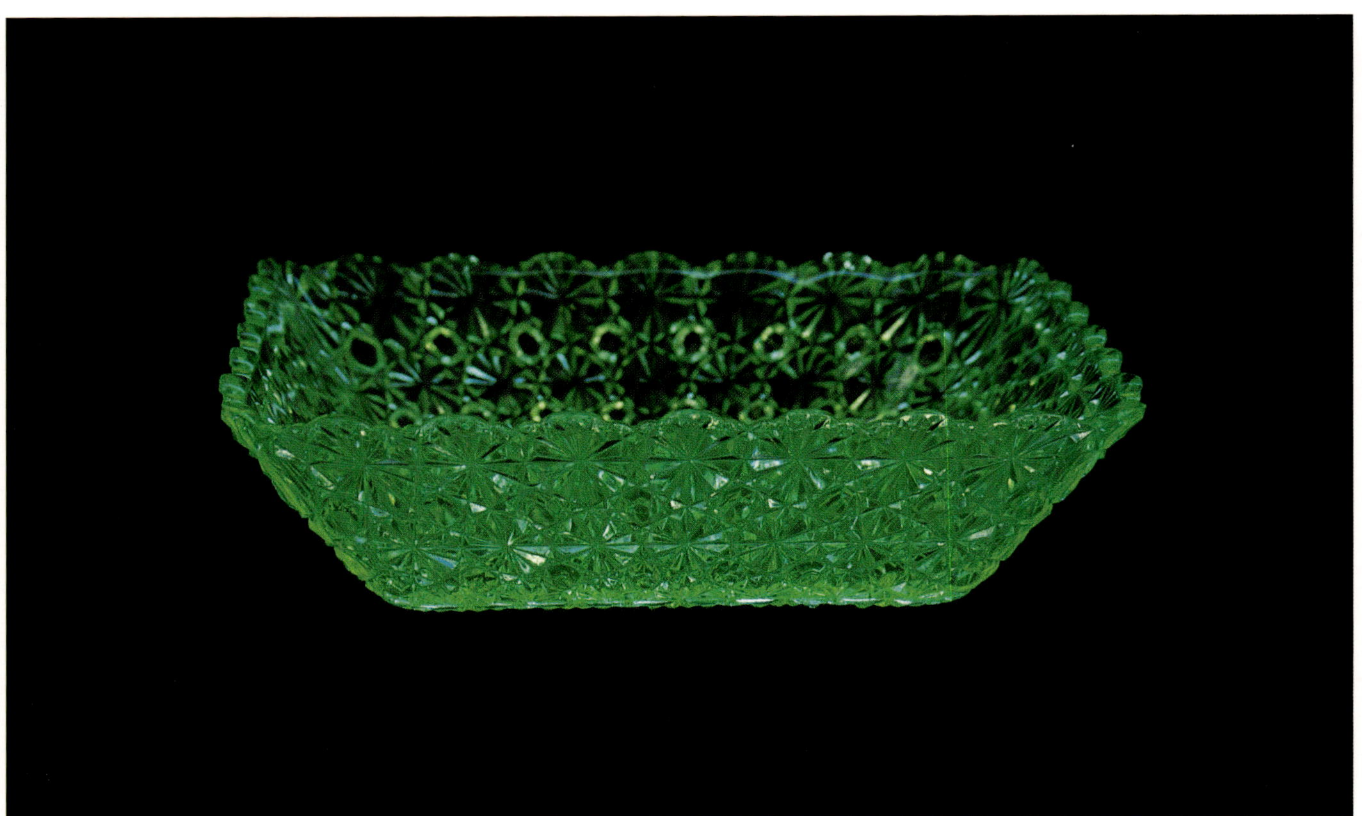

Rectangular bowl by U. S. Glass, c. 1890s. This *Daisy and Button* bowl measures 8.75"l x 5.75"w. $150-175

Rectangular bread tray made by U. S. Glass, c.1890s. This *Daisy and Button* tray is shaped like a sleigh and measures 11"l x 7"w. $150-175.

Water pitcher by Bryce Brothers, c.1890. *Daisy and Button* pitcher is 7.5"h. $450-500. Shown as part of a set on following page at top.

Water tray by U. S. Glass, c.1892. Clover shaped *Daisy and Button with V Ornament* water tray, 12"d. $200-250. Part of the set shown on the following page at top.

Opposite page, top:
Water set. The *Daisy and Button* 4"h tumbler is made by George
Duncan and Sons, c.1890s. $90-100. Pitcher and tray identified
above. Duncan and Bryce Brothers became part of U. S. Glass Co.

Opposite page, bottom:
Bowl and underplate with same *Daisy and Button* pattern as photo
below. Bowl is 3"h x 5.25"d and the underplate is 7.5"d. $350-400 set.

Covered compote maker unknown, c.1890s. The outside of the compote bowl and the inside of the
lid have the *Daisy and Button* pattern. The rim is scalloped and looped with a fan shaped panel
between each loop. 7.5"h. $300-350.

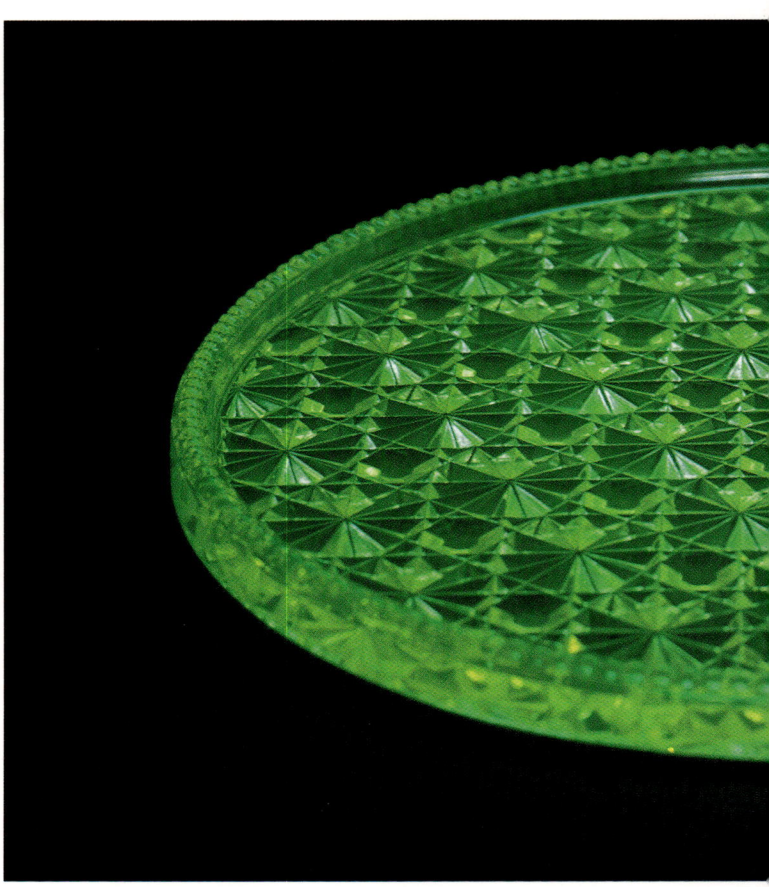

A *Daisy and Button with Thumbprint* cake stand, Adams and Co., c.1890. This high standard cake stand measures 7"h x 9.5"sq and was also referred to as a salver. $275-300.

Cheese and cover by Hobbs, Brockunier and Co., c.1885. This *Daisy and Button* cheese dish is 5"h x 7"d. $400-450.

Round cake plate possibly by U. S. Glass, c.1890s. This *Daisy and Button* cake plate is 12"d and has a beaded rim. $150-200.

Berry set by Bryce Brothers, c.1890. The pattern is *Daisy and Button* and the bowls have scalloped, pointed rims. Master berry, 4"h x 9.5"d. $300-350. Small berry, 2"h x 4.5"d. $75-95 ea.

Daisy and Button wine glasses by U. S. Glass, c.1890s. The design of these glasses is very sharp and distinct, 5.2"h x 2.6"d. $65-75 ea.

A cordial glass set made by Bryce Brothers, Richards and Hartley Glass Co., and U. S. Glass, c.1889-1891. This pattern is called *Finecut and Panel.* The cordials have 4 panels of finecut design alternating with 4 solid panels, 3.8"h x 2"d. $45-50 ea.

A group of *Daisy and Button* sauce bowls. Front row left, square bowl 1.5"h x 4.5"sq. Front row right, scalloped rim, round nappy, 1.25"h x 5"d. Back row left, nappy with sharp scalloped rim, 1.75" h x 4.5"d. Back row right, smooth scalloped rim nappy, 1.75"h x 5"d. All are made by U. S. Glass, c. 1890s. $70-80 ea.

Clover berry dishes by Richards and Hartley, c.1885. These dishes are very light in color, but glow as intensely as the darker colored glass. Two sizes are shown, 1.6"h x 4.5"d and 1.2"h x 3"d. $70-80 ea.

Daisy and Button butter pats and salt by U. S. Glass, c.1890s. The square butter pat is 2.6"sq, the triangle butter pat is 3"d. $45-65 ea. The salt is 1.75" h. $40-50ea.

A *Daisy and Button Crossbar* creamer, sugar bowl, and spooner. The table size creamer, sugar bowl, and spooner measure 5.75"h x 3.5"d, 8"h x 4.4"d, and 6"h x 3.8"d respectively. Creamer and spooner-$125-150 ea, sugar bowl-$150-195.

A *Daisy and Button Crossbar* ketchup cruet by Richard and Hartley, c.1885. This pattern originally called *Mikado* has not been reproduced. All pieces in this pattern are a very light canary color. This ketchup cruet is 8"h x 3.25"d. $250-275.

A *Daisy and Button Crossbar* compote. This high standard compote is 7.5"h x 8.5"d. $250-300.

A *Daisy and Button Crossbar* celery vase and milk pitcher. This celery vase is 7"h x 4.5"d. $250-275. The one quart milk pitcher is 6.25"h x 4.75"d. $350-400.

A *Daisy and Button Crossbar* creamer and finger bowl. This individual creamer is 2.8"h x 3.2"d. $100-125. The finger bowl is 3"h x 4"d. $125-175.

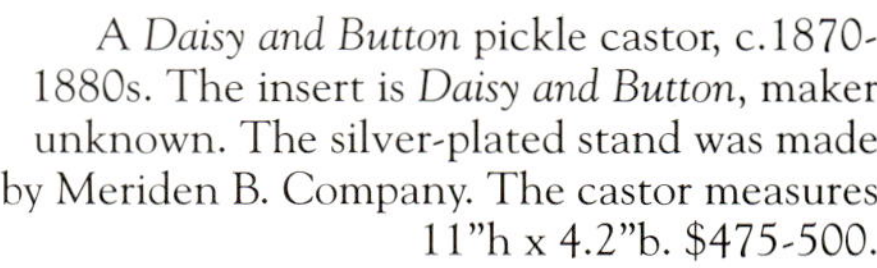

A *Daisy and Button* pickle castor, c.1870-1880s. The insert is *Daisy and Button*, maker unknown. The silver-plated stand was made by Meriden B. Company. The castor measures 11"h x 4.2"b. $475-500.

A *Paneled Daisy and Button* punch set by Duncan, c.1890s. This high standard punch bowl is 11"h x 9.5"d. $625-650, and the cups are 2.25"h x 3"d. $80-95 ea.

A *Paneled Daisy and Button* bowl by Duncan, c.1890s. This large fruit bowl with its pointed and scalloped top is 5.75"h x 11.25"d. $375-425.

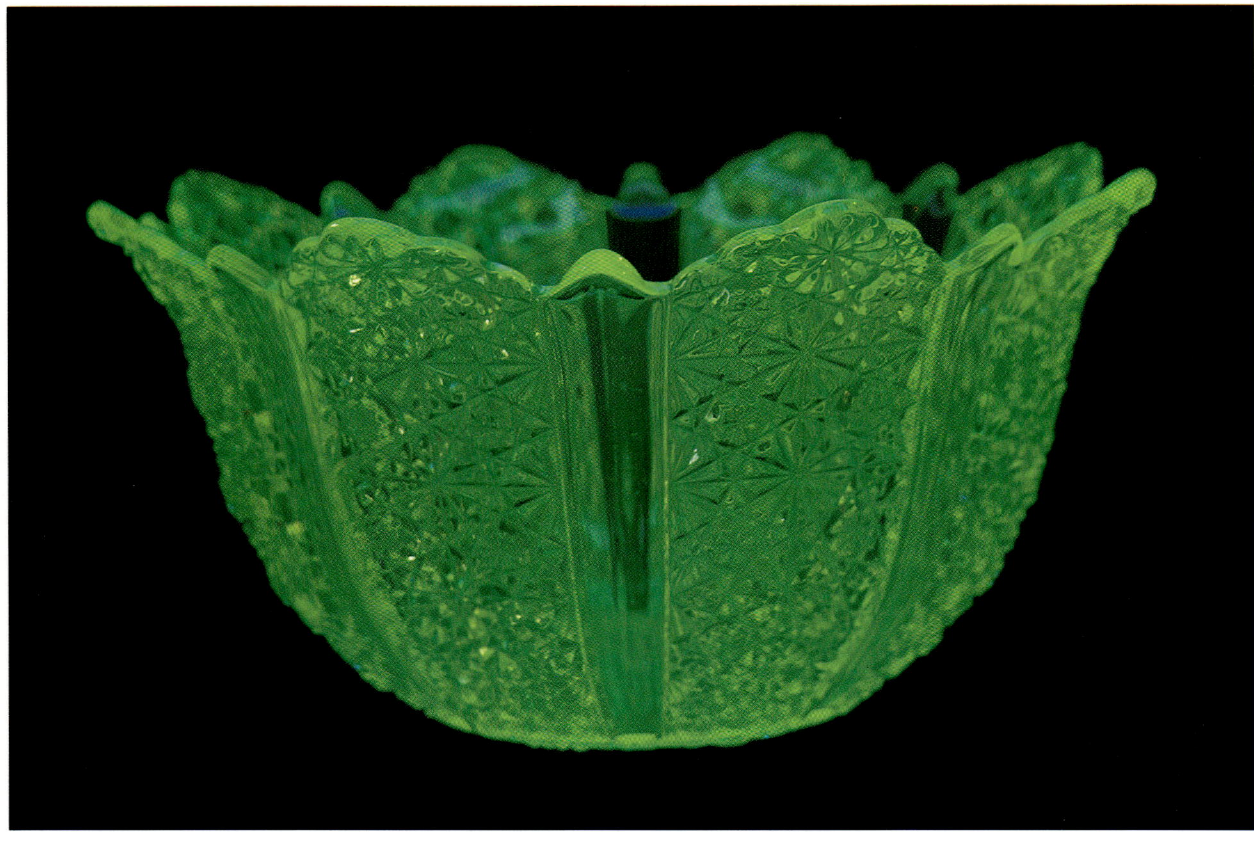

A *Daisy and Button* pickle castor, maker unknown, c.1880s. The insert is in the *Daisy and Button* pattern, the stand is silver-plate, 10.25"h x 4.7"b. $350-385.

Pickle castor. The maker of the diamond design insert is unknown. The silver-plated stand is marked Pairpoint, c.1880s, 11"h x 3.75"b. $375-395. *Courtesy of Laura Kelm and Pete Buck.*

Daisy and Button pickle castor, maker unknown, c.1880s. This *Daisy and Button* insert is in a silver-plated stand, 10.75"h. $475-500. *Courtesy of Laura Kelm and Pete Buck.*

A *Daisy and Button* castor set, maker unknown, c.1880s. This 5 bottle castor set has Vaseline, blue, amber, and clear *Daisy and Button* bottles in a clear *Daisy and Button* holder, 10.5"h x 5"b. $525-575.

Castor set, maker unknown, c.1870-1880s. The bottles of this 4 bottle set have a band of acid etched leaves around the centers. The clear stopper is not original. The stand is silver-plate, 10"h x 5.5"b. $500-550.

Daisy and Button boot and slipper. The *Daisy and Button* boot by Duncan and Sons, c.1880s, is 4.25"h x 4.75"l. The distinguishing characteristics of this boot are the laces and lace holes on the front panel. Unlike the original novelty, the reproduction is plain. It also has a hollow sole and solid heel with a scalloped top edge. $75-95. The *Daisy and Button* slipper has an open front with a solid heel and mesh sole. Possibly by Duncan, c.1880s. 2.75"h x 5.75"l. $65-85. *Courtesy of Laura Kelm and Pete Buck.*

Daisy and Button slipper by Duncan, c.1887. 1.75"h x 3.25"l. $80-90.

A 5 bottle castor set, c.1870-1880s.
The bottles of this castor set are *Daisy and Button* pattern, maker unknown.
The circular silver-plated stand on a high stem rotates around the looped handle. The stand is marked with Derby Silver Co. Derby, Conn. and is 16.5"h x 7.25"b. $650-700.

Two Bryce Brothers shoes, c.1880s. The *Daisy and Button* slipper has a V shaped open front and is 1.9"h x 4.7"l. $75-85. The *Cane* pattern slipper is 1.75"h x 4.75"l. This pointed-toe slipper is called a "Chinese" shoe. $85-95. *Courtesy of Laura Kelm and Pete Buck.*

These are old *Daisy and Button* shoes. The *Daisy and Button Skate* was made by Central Glass Company, c.1870-1885. It has not been reproduced. It is 3.25"h x 5.5"l. $75-85. The *Daisy and Button Bootie* was made by Duncan and Sons, c.1897. It is 2.4"h x 4.25"l. $65-75. The *Daisy and Button Slipper* on the right was made by Duncan, c.1886. It is 2.3"h x 5"l and has an advertisement on the bottom *"Sollers and Co. Fine Shoes"*. $85-90.

The photo above shows the ad on the sole of the slipper.

A group of *Daisy and Button* pieces identified left to right. The *Daisy and Button* barrel toothpick holder (toothpick) by U. S. Glass, c.1890s, is 2.6"h x 2"d. $60-75. The *Fashion* toothpick by U. S. Glass/ Richards and Hartley, c.1890-1892 is 2.4"h x 2.4"d. $45-55. The *Daisy and Button* toothpick or match holder by Duncan, c.1890 is 2.65"h x 2.4"d. $50-65. The *Daisy and Button* cup by McKee, c.1886 is 2.1"h x 2.7"d and was called a Venice lemonade. $50-65.

A *Daisy and Button with V Ornament* toothpick by U. S. Glass, c.1892. This pattern has not been reproduced. The toothpick is 2.1"h x 2"w. $75-90. *Courtesy of Bill McFarling.*

A *Daisy and Button* salt shaker, maker unknown, c.1890s. 3.65"h x 1.7"d. $50-60.

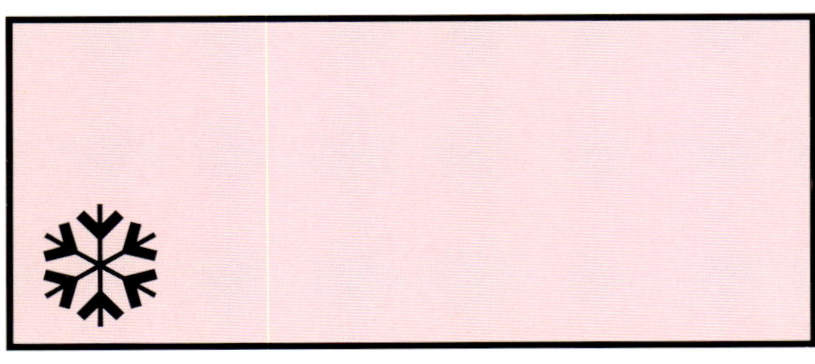

A sandwich tray by Richards and Hartley Glass Co., c.1890s. This 10" plate was originally referred to as a salver. This is Hartley's No. 900 pattern. It is a very light canary color. $125-150.

A *Daisy and Button* platter possibly U.S. Glass, c.1890s. This large, 2 handled platter is 11"l x 9"w. $250-275.

A *Daisy and Button* bowl by Hobbs, Brockunier and Co., c.1885. Notice how this bowl is shaped like a bassinet, 9.75"l x 6.4w. $175-200.

Clio bowl by Challinor, Taylor and Co., c.1890. This 10" shallow bowl is the *Clio* pattern instead of plain *Daisy and Button* according to Glickman. $275-300.

Boat by Bryce Brothers, c.1890s. This boat, perhaps used as a salt, is referred to as "Earl ind. boat" in U. S. Glass From A to Z, page 80. It is 1"h x 4.5"l x 1.65"w. $125-150. *Courtesy of Laura Kelm and Pete Buck.*

Daisy and Button plate by Bryce Brothers, c.1890. This pattern was originally called *"Fashion,"* 7"sq. $65-85.

A *Daisy and Button* bowl by U. S. Glass, c.1890s. This large boat shaped bowl is 12"l x 7.75"w. $375-400.

Clio dinner plate by Challinor, Taylor and Co., c.1890. This dinner plate is 10"d and has a scalloped rim. $80-95.

Daisy and Button water tray by Hobbs, c.1885. This clover leaf water tray is 12.75"d. $200-250. *Courtesy of Laura Kelm and Pete Buck.*

A *Daisy and Button* bowl by U. S. Glass, c.1890s. This large fruit bowl is 4.25"h x 10.75"d. $350-425. *Courtesy of Bill McFarling.*

A *Medallion* compote, maker unknown, c.1885-1895. This high standard compote design is unusual in that it is on the outside of the bowl and the inside of the cover. 11.75"h x 8"d. $350-395.

A *Medallion* goblet. This is a 6 oz. goblet, 6.25"h. $115-125.

A *Medallion* cake stand. This high standard cake stand is 6.5"h x 10"d. $325-350.

A barber bottle, maker unknown, c.1890s. This pattern is very similar to several of the early pressed glass patterns, however, I have been unable to identify it exactly. For the purpose of this book, I have called it *Zippered Star*. 8.75"h x 4"d. $175-200.

A *Zippered Star* ring holder, 2.5"h x 3.5"d. $45-65. *Courtesy of Laura Kelm and Pete Buck.*

A *Zippered Star* cologne bottle, 6.5"h x 2.25"d. $225-250. *Courtesy of Laura Kelm and Pete Buck.*

Quilted Diamond tray and salts, maker unknown, c.1880s. This pattern is also referred to as *Diamond Quilted*. The cracker tray is 1.5"h x 7.75"l x 4.5"w. with the diamond pattern on the inside of the sides and the outside of the bottom. The salts are 1"h x 2.25"l x 1.5"w. $85 ea. *Courtesy of Laura Kelm and Pete Buck.*

A *Quilted Diamond* celery vase. This celery vase is 8.75"h x 4.2"b. $175-200.

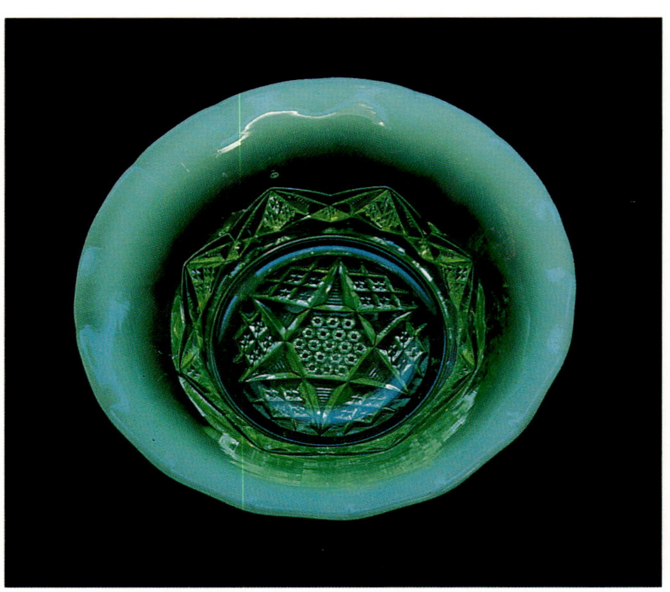

A *Diamond Spearhead* bowl by Northwood, c.1900. This opalescent bowl is one of my favorites with its crisp design. It has not been reproduced. 2.75"h x 7.75"d. $165-195.

A *Diamond Spearhead* spooner, toothpick, and jelly compote. The spooner is 4.35" x 3.34"d. $170-200. The toothpick is 2.5"h. $130-150. The jelly compote is 4.5"h x 4.15"d. $165-190.

A *Ribbed Spiral* bowl by Model Flint, c.1902, and Northwood, c.1903. This very attractive pattern has not been reproduced, 2.5"h x 8"d. $175-195. *Courtesy of Bill McFarling.*

A *Ribbed Spiral* spooner, toothpick, and creamer. The spooner is 4.1"h x 3.9"d. $95-125. The creamer is 4.1"h x 3.1"d. $95-125. The toothpick is 2.4"h x 2"d. $170-195. *Courtesy of Bill McFarling.*

Swag with Brackets water set by Jefferson Glass Co., c.1904. This pattern has not been reproduced in opalescent. The pitcher is 8"h x 5.75"d. $400-450. The tumblers are 6 oz. and 4"h x 2.95"d. $95-100 ea.

Swag with Brackets jelly compotes. These compotes are slightly different. The slightly ruffled rim is almost smooth on one of them suggesting a worn mold, 5.25"h x 4.5"d. $95-120 ea.

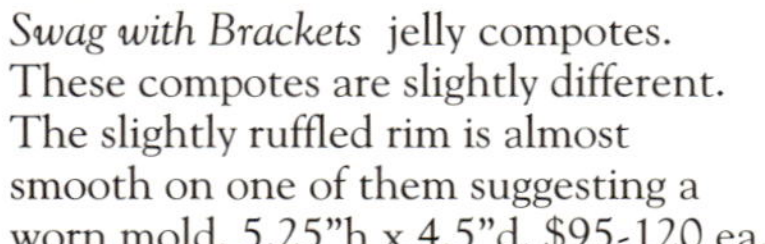

Above right and right: *Question Marks* compote by Dugan, c.1900s. Two views are shown of this very unusual compote to demonstrate the combination of its 3 patterns. The *Question Marks* pattern is on the inside, the *Georgia Belle* pattern is on the outside, and the *Puzzle* pattern is on the foot. 3"h x 6"d. $165-195.

Wreath and Shell water set by Model Flint Glass Co., c.1900-1903. This pattern has not been reproduced, and its collectibility is very good. It is sometimes decorated with flowers. The pitcher is 8.5"h x 4.2"b. $400-450. The flat footed, 6 oz. tumblers are 3.75"h x 2.9"d. $95-120 ea. Courtesy of Lois and Larry Smith.

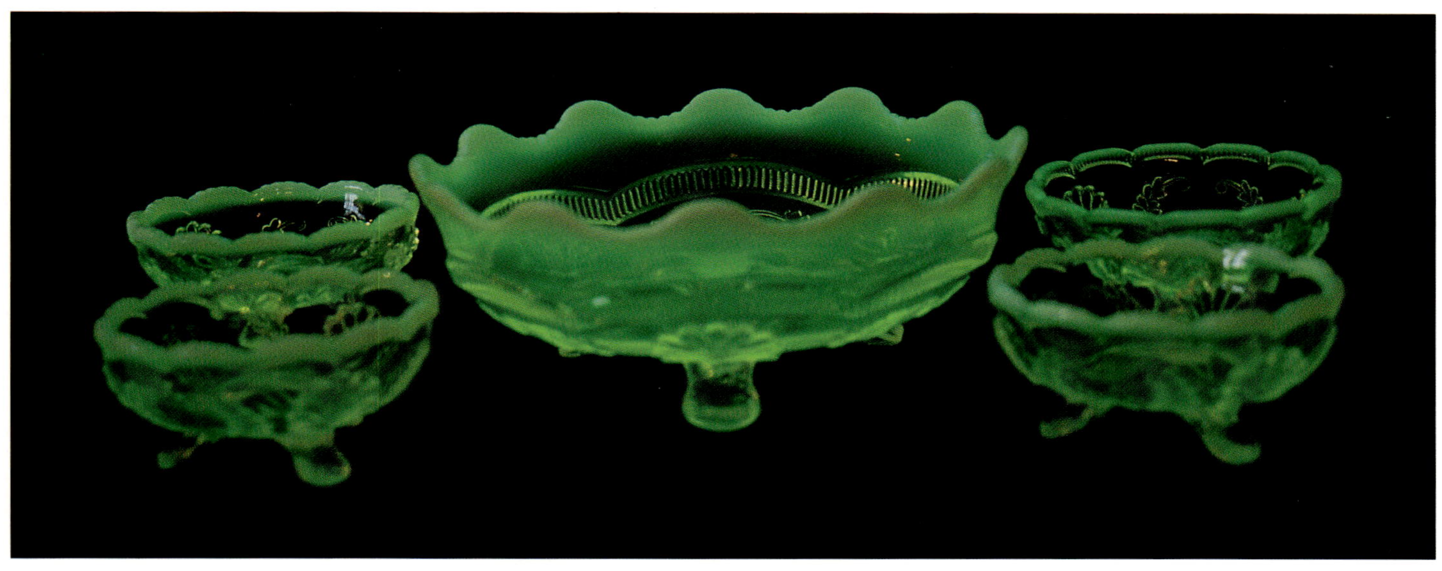

Wreath and Shell berry set. These bowls are 3 footed. The master berry bowl is 3.75" x 8.25"d. $250-300. The sauce bowls are 2.15"h x 4.3"d. $50-65 ea. *Courtesy of Lois and Larry Smith.*

Wreath and Shell rose bowl. This opalescent rose bowl is 4.25"h x 3.5"d. $140-190.

Wreath and Shell sugar bowl. This large sugar bowl is 5.25"h x 4"d. $250-275.

Wreath and Shell spooner. This spooner is an example of *Wreath and Shell* decorated with flowers, 4.5"h x 3.5"d. $165-185.

Wreath and Shell butter dish, 5.5"h x 7.25"d. $350-375.

Wreath and Shell salt dip. This tiny salt dip measures 1.35"h x 1.8"d. $125-140.

Wreath and Shell spittoons. A pair of lady's spittoons 4.5"h x 3.45"d. $200-225 ea.

A *Spanish Lace* water pitcher by Northwood, c.1899. This pattern is very collectible. The pitcher has a smooth applied handle and ruffled top, 9.25"h. $600-650.

A *Spanish Lace* bowl. This crimped top novelty bowl is 3.5"h x 8"l x 5.9"w. $225-250. *Courtesy of Laura Kelm and Pete Buck.*

Inverted Fan and Feather spittoon by National/Duncan, c.1901. Women of the Victorian Era reportedly utilized these small spittoons and concealed them in their flowing dress sleeves. This very attractive spittoon is 4.75"h x 3"d. $300-350.

Iris with Meander tumblers by Jefferson Glass Co., c.1903. This pattern has not been reproduced. These two, 6 oz. opalescent tumblers appear to be made from different molds as one is flared at the top and the other is straight. They measure 3.65"h and 3.8"h respectively. $100-125 ea.

Above and right:
An *Argonaut Shell* novelty dish by The Northwood Co., c.1889-1910. Two views are shown in order to demonstrate the shell-like pattern. 3.5"h x 6.75"d, 3.2"b. $125-150.

Northwood Block
novelty bowl.
$150-175. *Courtesy of Melanie Schonier.*

A *Northwood Block* celery vase by
Northwood Glass, c.1905. This
opalescent celery vase is 6"h x 4.45"d x
3.65"b. $125-175.

A *Fluted Scrolls* spooner by The Northwood Co., c.1898-
1900s. This pattern also referred to as *Klondyke* and as
Jackson has not been reproduced. It is sometimes
decorated with an enameled band of daisies and gold.
This spooner is 4.25"h x 4"d. $140-150. *Courtesy of
Laura Kelm and Pete Buck.*

Fluted Scrolls creamer and sugar. The
creamer is 4.5"h x 4"d. $125-150. The
sugar is 6.75"h x 4.8"d. $175-225.

Fluted Scrolls butter dishes. The large butter dish measures 6"h x 7"d. $300-350. The quarter-pound butter dish is 4.5"h x 5.25"d. This piece was also referred to as a powder or puff jar. Notice the daisies on the bowl. $225-250.

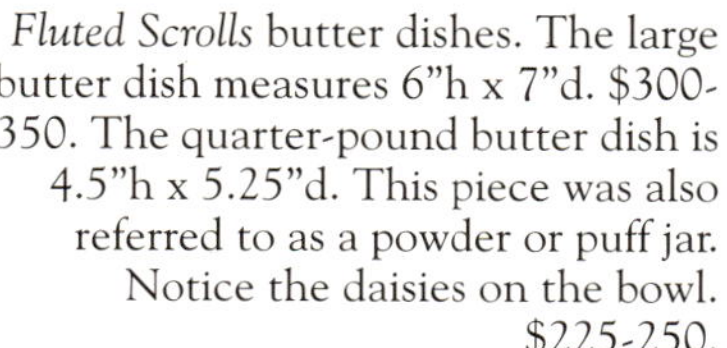

Fluted Scrolls cruet and shaker set. The cruet is 4.5"h x 3.5"d. $200-250. The salt and pepper shakers are also used with the *Alaska* pattern, 2.8"h x 2.25"d. $100-125 ea.

Fluted Scrolls novelty bowl is 3.5"h x 7"d. $100-125. *Courtesy of Laura Kelm and Pete Buck.*

Fluted Scrolls berry set. The master berry is 3.3"h x 8.75"d. $250-300. The sauce bowls are 1.7"h x 5.25"d. $75-95 ea.

Fluted Scrolls water set decorated with an enameled band of daisies and gold. The tumblers are interchangeable with the *Alaska* pattern. The difference in the decorated items is the type of flower used. The *Alaska* pattern would have forget-me-nots with elephant ears. The 6 oz. tumbler is 3.75"h. $100-125 ea. The pitcher is 7.5"h. $500-550.

Left:
An *Alaska* butter dish by The Northwood Co., c.1897. This pattern has not been reproduced and is very collectible. It is sometimes decorated with enameled forget-me-not flowers and elephant ear leaves, with or without gold. This decorated butter dish is 4.75"h x 6.75"sq. $400-450.

Center:
An *Alaska* creamer and spooner. These pieces are 3.2"h x 3.9"sq. $140-165 ea.

Bottom:
An *Alaska* celery tray, 2.4"h x 9.5"l x 4.3"w. $190-200.

Twig vases by Northwood Glass, c.1910. This pattern has been reproduced in both sizes. The reproductions have solid branches at the base. The large vase is 7"h x 2.75"b. $150-185. The small twig vase is 4.5"h x 2.25"b. $100-125.

Alaska sauce dishes. This pair of decorated sauces measure 1.9"h x 3.75"sq. $90-130 ea.

An *Opal Open* vase by Northwood, c.1910. This pattern is also known as *Beaded Panels*. This pattern has been reproduced. The reproduction has a solid stem. 5.4"h x 3.45"d x 3.2"b. $175-200.

Corn vase by Northwood-Dugan, c.1905. This pattern has been reproduced. The reproduction has a smooth top. The corn kernels and shucks of this opalescent vase are very distinct, 8"h x 2.5"b. $185-200.

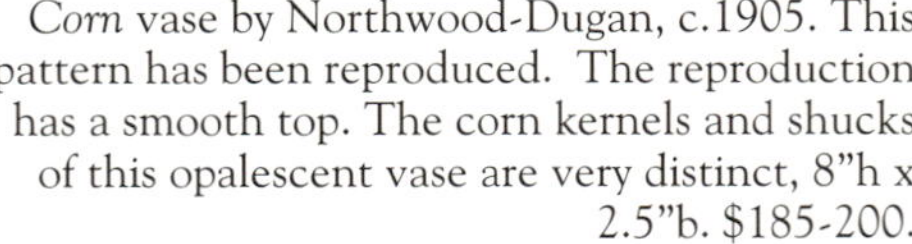

Corn vases. Notice the difference in the shapes of the tops, the distinction of the corn kernels, and the degree of opalescence. The left vase is 8.5"h and the right is 8"h. $185-200. *Courtesy of Laura Kelm and Pete Buck.*

Pump and Trough by Northwood Glass Co., c.1907. This pattern has been reproduced. The reproduction pump has a smooth top. This pump is 6.5"h x 3.6"b. $120-150. This trough is 2.15"h x 5.1"l x 2.6"w. $60-95.

A *Cactus* celery vase by Indiana Tumbler and Goblet, c.1900-1903. This opalescent vase is 7"h x 3.2"b. $200-225.

A *Jack-in-Pulpit* vase by Model Flint Glass Co., c.1902. This is the *Lorna* pattern, 6.75"h x 2.75"b. $150-175.

Hexagonal bowl, maker unknown, c.1900s. This simple but pretty hexagonal shaped opalescent bowl with a smooth ground bottom is 6.5"d. $100-125. *Courtesy of Laura Kelm and Pete Buck.*

Three Panel bowl by Richards and Hartley Glass Co., c.1891. The pattern on this bowl consists of three button pattern panels separated by three double bar panels, 3.75"h x 7.5"d. $150-175.

A *Button Panels* bowl by Coudersport Tile and Ornamental Glass Co., c.1903. This bowl is 2.75"h x 6.75"d. $125-150. *Courtesy of Laura Kelm and Pete Buck.*

Pearls and Scales compote by Northwood Glass Co., c.1905. This compote's name describes it well, 3.65"h x 6.25"d. $125-150.

A *Barbells* bowl by Jefferson Glass Co., c.1905. This pretty opalescent bowl is photographed upside down to show the distinctive bars and bull's-eyes design which resemble barbells, thus the pattern name. 3.5"h x 7.25"d. $124-145.

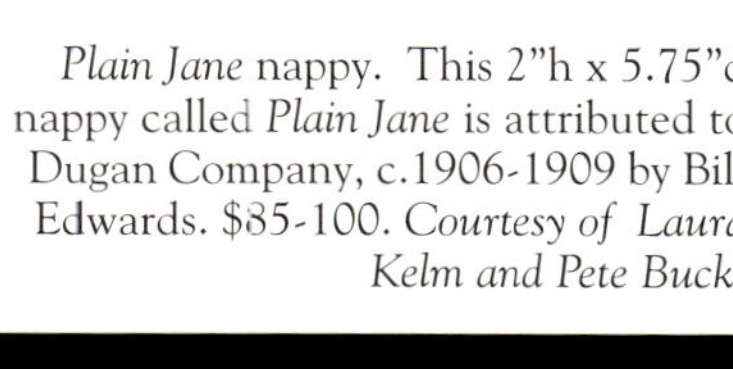

Plain Jane nappy. This 2"h x 5.75"d nappy called *Plain Jane* is attributed to Dugan Company, c.1906-1909 by Bill Edwards. $85-100. *Courtesy of Laura Kelm and Pete Buck.*

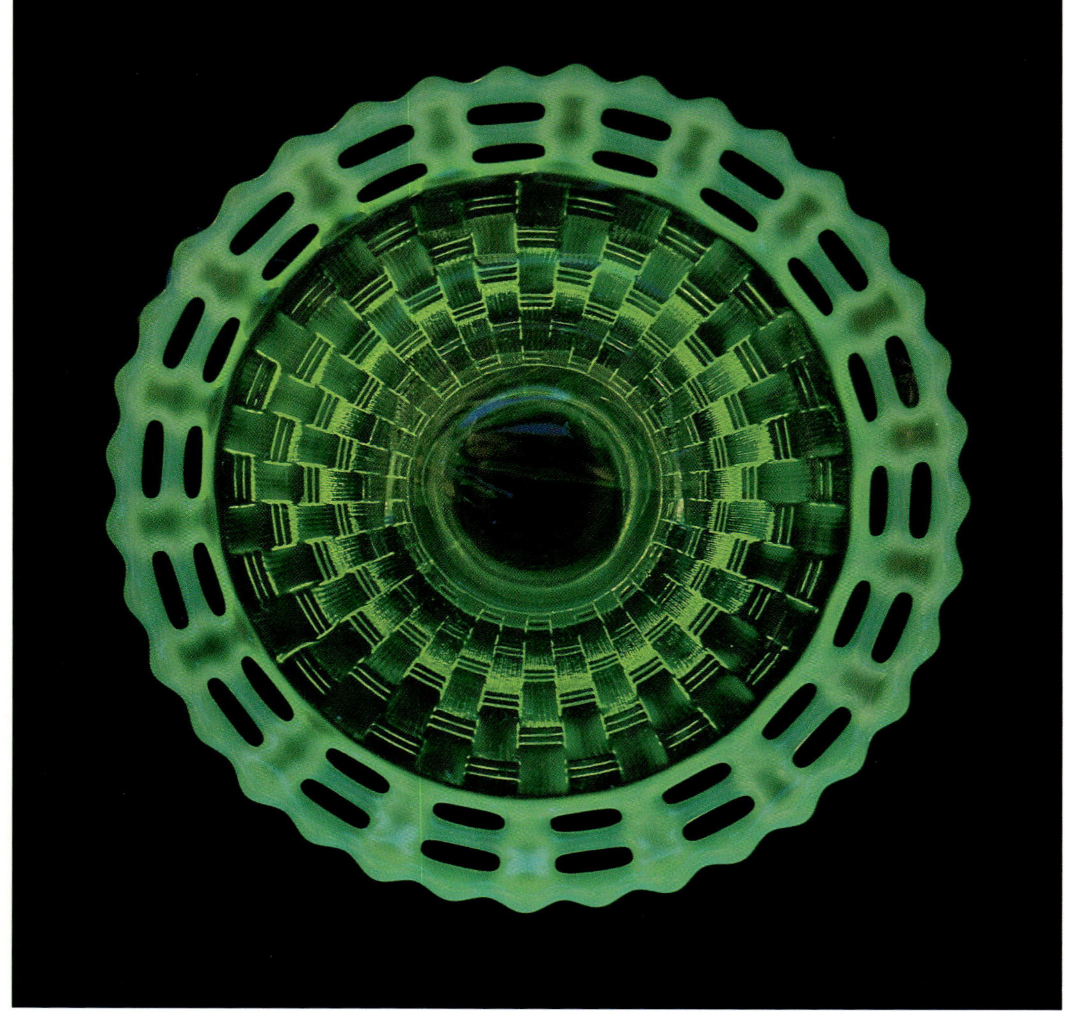

A *Fenton Basketweave* bowl, c.1911. The bases of bowls of this pattern look like woven baskets. The opalescent edge is open. 1.8"h x 6.8"d. $65-75. *Courtesy of Laura Kelm and Pete Buck.*

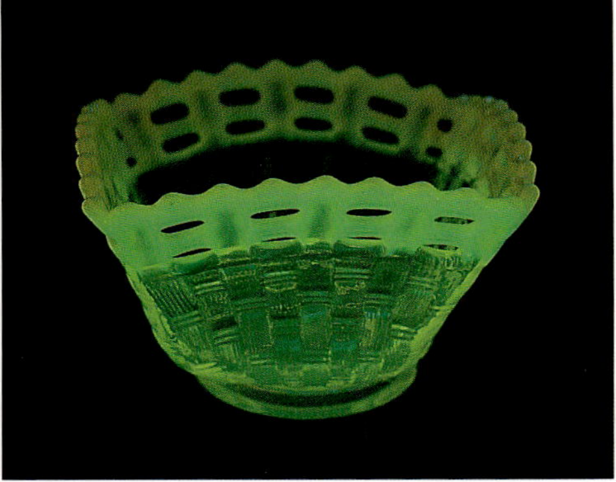

A *Fenton Basketweave* bowl, 3.2"h x 4.75"w. $65-75.

Over-All Hob tumbler by Nickel Plate Glass and U. S. Glass, c.1892. This 6 oz. tumbler has very heavy opalescence and is 4"h x 3"d. $95-100.

A set of *Reverse Swirl* salt and pepper shakers by Buckeye Glass Co. and Model Flint Glass Co., c.1888-1890. These opalescent shakers are 2.5"h. No two pieces have the exact same pattern. $100-115 ea.

Two pairs of salt and pepper shakers. The maker of the salt and pepper on the left is unknown, c.1870s. The pattern is *Daisy and Button* with a double crossbar. The shakers have zinc tops and are 3.5"h. Reported as rare in vaseline by Glickman. $160-175 ea. The salt and pepper on the right is *Dewey* by Indiana Tumbler and Goblet Co., c.1898. They are 3"h. $100-115 ea.

Dewey sugar bowls by Indiana Tumbler and Goblet Co., c.1898. This table size sugar without a lid is 4"d. $150-175. The individual sugar without a lid is 2.5"d. $125-150. *Courtesy of Laura Kelm and Pete Buck.*

Rose Sprig sleigh salt. This pretty little salt has a rose design on the side and is 2"h x 3"l x 1.75"w. $65-75. *Courtesy of Laura Kelm and Pete Buck.*

Dew Drop creamer and mug by La Belle Glass Company, c.1886. This four footed creamer is 4.75"h x 4.4"w. $100-125. The mug is pictured in a 1889 Butler Bros. catalogue. It is 2.9"h x 2.7"d. $50-75.

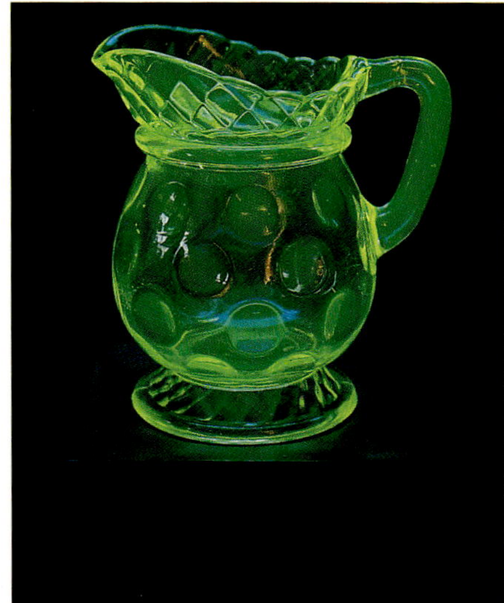

A *Lattice and Thumbprint* creamer by Central Glass, c.1880s. This thumbprint design creamer is 4.25"h x 3.2"d. $125-175.

Rose Sprig compote by Campbell, Jones, and Co., c.1886. This high standard compote has a scalloped top and a rose design on the side, 5.25"h x 7"d. $150-175.

A geometric design creamer, maker unknown (possibly Sandwich), c.1860s. This little creamer is a blown 3 part mold. The top third is reverse swirls, the 2nd third is diamond design, and the bottom third is a sunburst design. The applied handle is clear. 4.4"h x 3.3"d. $275-300.

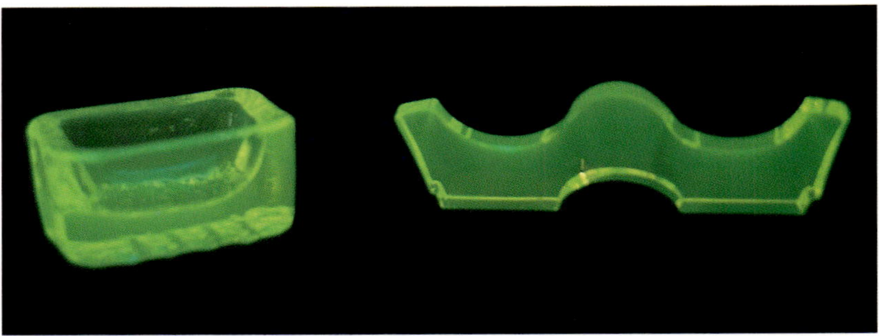

A knife rest and salt. The maker of this double knife rest is unknown, c.1890s. It is 4.1"l, $95-115. The salt is *Heavy Paneled Finecut* by Duncan, c.1890. It is 1.1"h x 2.25"l x 1.6"w. $90-110. *Courtesy of Larry and Lois Smith.*

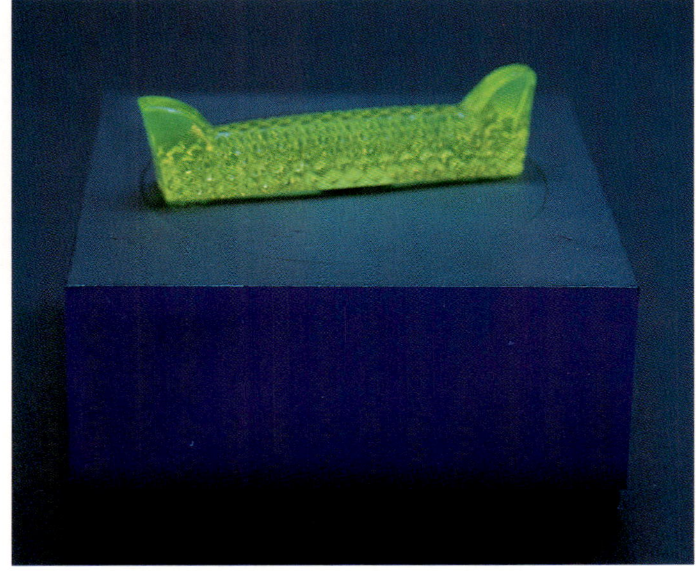

A knife rest, maker unknown, c.1890s. This knife rest measures 2.8"l x .5"w. $125-145.

Beaumont's Columbia creamer, sugar, and spooner by Beaumont Glass Co., c.1898. These pieces are trimmed in gold. Creamer is 4.2"h x 3.65"d, $160-190; sugar is 6.75"h x 3.95"d, $200-225; spooner is 4.25"h x 3.5"d, $160-190.

Beaumont's Columbia butter dish, 5.5"h x 7.5"d. $325-350.

Lorne butter dish and cover by Bryce Brothers, c.1890s. This unusual covered butter dish was probably not part of a larger matching table service. 3.75"h x 7"l x 5"w. $300-325.

A *Holly Clear* butter dish by Indiana Tumbler and Goblet, c.1903. This butter dish has a conical domed cover with plain vertical panels alternating with panels with a holly pattern. The panels are outlined in rows of beads, 5.75"h x 7.5"d. $450-500. *Courtesy of Lois and Larry Smith.*

A *Clio* butter dish by Challinor, Taylor and Co., c.1890. This *Daisy and Button*-like patterned butter dish is 6.25"h x 6.75"d. $475-525. *Courtesy of Lois and Larry Smith.*

Left and below:
This *Leaf* flanged butter by Bryce Brothers, c.1890s, is not part of a complete table service. Notice the leaf design and the butterfly, 4.75"h x 7"d. Two views are shown for detail. $450-500. *Courtesy of Lois and Larry Smith.*

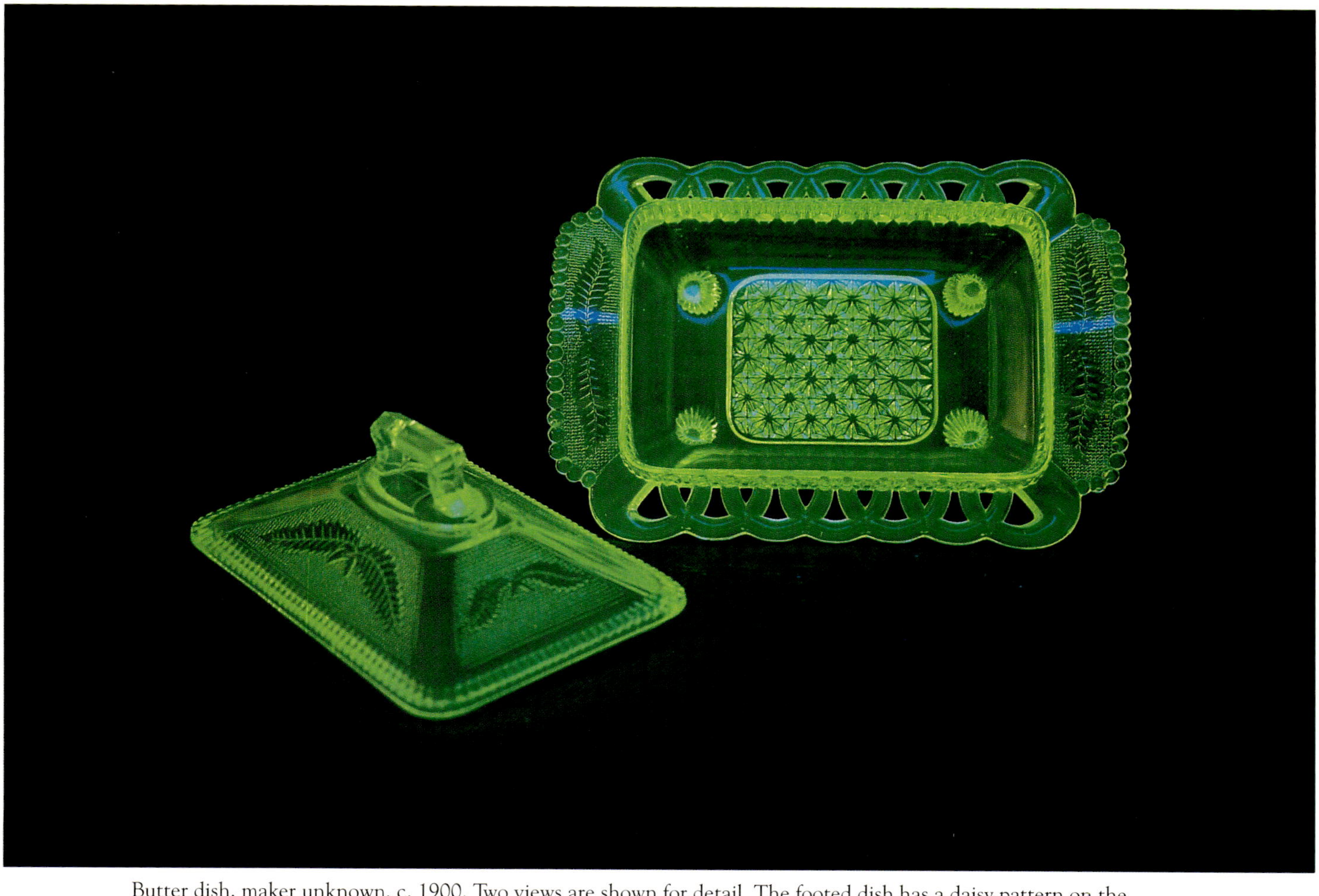

Butter dish, maker unknown, c. 1900. Two views are shown for detail. The footed dish has a daisy pattern on the bottom side, the sides have a looped trim, and the ends are curved with beaded rims and a leaf design on the bottom sides. The lid has the leaf pattern on the inside. 4"h x 7.75"l x 5.5"w. $250-300.

Basketweave water tray, maker unknown, c. 1880s. Notice the rural design in the center of this 12"d water tray. $200-225. *Courtesy of Laura Kelm and Pete Buck.*

Wildflower water tray by Adams and Co., c.1874. This oval tray is 13"l x 11"w. $175-225. *Courtesy of Laura Kelm and Pete Buck.*

Basketweave water pitcher, maker unknown, c.1880s. This half-gallon water pitcher is 8.25"h x 5.25"d. $250-300. *Courtesy of Laura Kelm and Pete Buck.*

Lattice and Daisy water set by Duncan, c.1912. The opalescence of these tumblers has red highlights in this photo instead of the usual translucent bluish-white, due to the strong rays of the light. The pitcher is 9.5"h x 5"d. $400-450. The tumblers are 4.2"h x 2.9"d. $90-125 ea.

Below:
Striped water set, maker possibly Fenton, c. unknown. This opalescent striped pitcher is 8.25"h x 3.9"b. $450-500. The matching tumblers are 5"h x 2.9"d. $95-105. *Courtesy of Larry and Lois Smith.*

Maple Leaf plate by Gillander and Sons, c.1885. This 10"d plate has a diamond center with maple leaf border. This pattern has not been reproduced in canary. $75-100. *Courtesy of Larry and Lois Smith.*

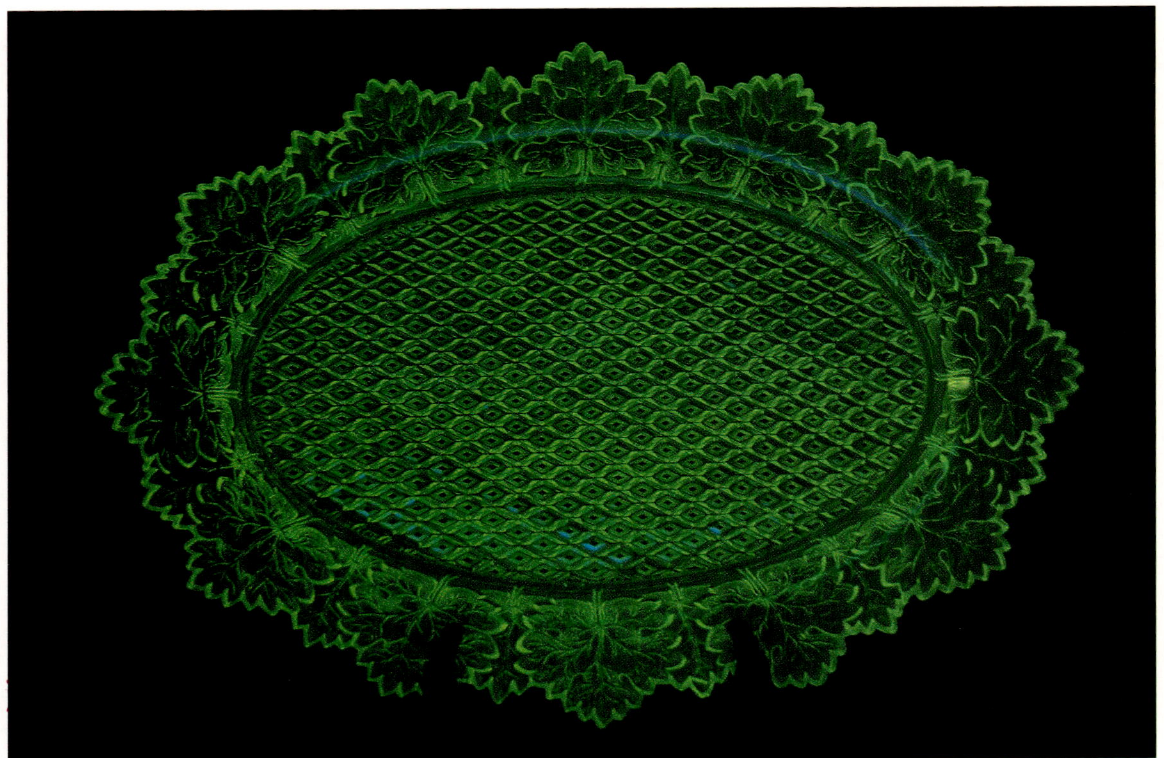

A *Maple Leaf* bread tray. This oval tray is 13.75"l x 9.5"w and has a diamond pattern center and maple leaf edge. $125-150.

A *Maple Leaf* bowl. This oval fruit bowl is covered with maple leaves and the 4 feet have a bark-like pattern, 4"h x 9.75"l x 6"w. $175-225.

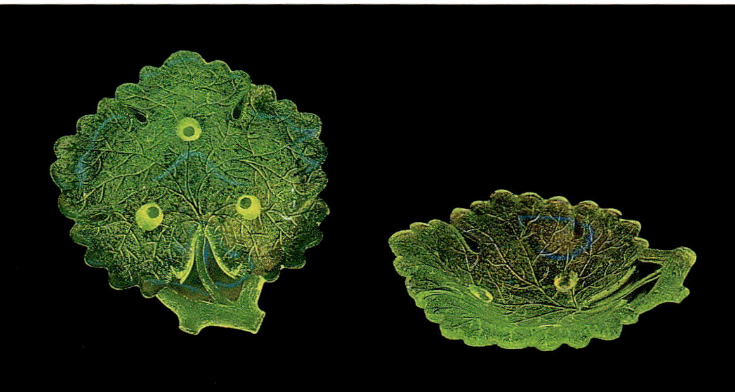

Maple Leaf sauce dishes. These sauce dishes are 3 footed individual maple leaves, 1.2"h x 4"d. $35-55 ea.

Leaf Mold salt and pepper, and toothpick by Northwood, c.1894. This pattern is shown here in red spatter canary or white and cranberry cased with canary. The salt and pepper are 2.6"h x 2.35"d, $110-120 ea. The top of this toothpick has unfortunately been ground, 1.85"h x 2.45"d. $190-195.

An *Old Man Winter* basket by Jefferson Company, c.1902. This large footed basket with looped handle is 7"h x 7.75"d. $300-350. *Courtesy of Larry and Lois Smith.*

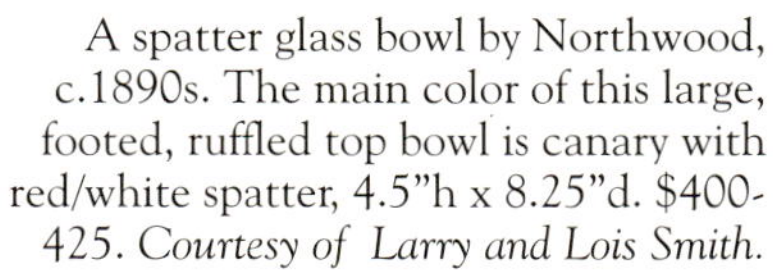

A spatter glass bowl by Northwood, c.1890s. The main color of this large, footed, ruffled top bowl is canary with red/white spatter, 4.5"h x 8.25"d. $400-425. *Courtesy of Larry and Lois Smith.*

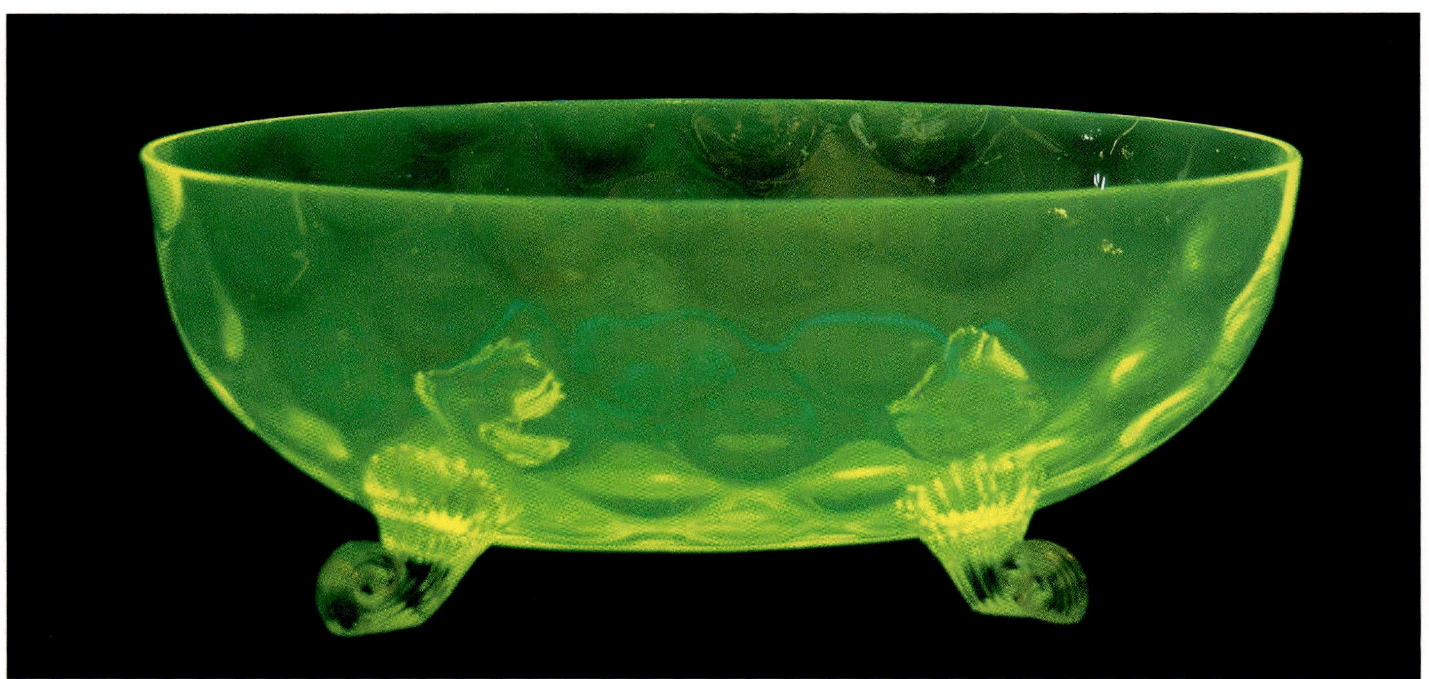

Inverted Thumbprint fruit bowl, maker unknown, c.1890s. The feet on this large footed fruit bowl resemble those of the pattern *Fluted Scrolls*. It is 4.5"h x 11.5"l x 7.25"w. $325-350. *Courtesy of Larry and Lois Smith.*

A *Rubina Verde* tumbler by Hobbs, c.1885. This 8 oz. tumbler is 3.75"h x 2.6"d. $125-145. *Courtesy of Laura Kelm and Pete Buck.*

A Victorian pin tray, maker unknown, c.1890s. This fan shaped pin tray is 9"l x 6"w and is trimmed in gold. $150-195.

Large vase, maker and circa unknown. This large vase has a thumbprint pattern and is 9.75"h x 7.5"w. $225-250. *Courtesy of Laura Kelm and Pete Buck.*

A *Single Lily Spool* epergne by Jefferson
Glass, c.1890s. This epergne is 8"h.
$225-250. *Courtesy of Laura Kelm and
Pete Buck.*

A swirl vase maker and circa unknown.
This fluted vase with a reverse swirl
type pattern is 5.5"h x 5"d. $225-250.
Courtesy of Laura Kelm and Pete Buck.

A celery vase by Northwood/ Dugan,
c.1895. This unusual flared top celery
vase was decorated with a treatment
using colored frit. Very hard to detect
in this photo are the light blue flecks.
The vase is 6.25"h x 4"d. $110-135.

An *External Ribs* vase by Hobbs,
Brockunier and Co. Glass, c.1885. This
External Ribs pattern vase is made with
two plated colors, canary outside with
gold spangles and white inside. It is
5.5"h x 5.25"d. $200-250.

Rose Bowl. This cased glass, white and canary, rose bowl has applied leaves in canary and applied flowers in cranberry. The maker is unknown, c.1890s. $350-375. *Courtesy of Melanie Schonier.*

Hobbs Basket made by Hobbs, Brockunier, c.1870s. This beautiful canary opalescent ribbed basket has a clear crystal looped handle and applied cranberry flowers, 7.5"h x 4.85"d. $325-365. *Courtesy of Bill McFarling.*

Hobbs lamp. The base of this ribbed opalescent glass lamp rests on a very ornate brass stand. The round top plate of the stand is attached to the 6.5" square bottom plate by 4 legs. The sides of the square plate have a filigree flower design. The applied flowers are pink and cranberry with vaseline centers. The stems are clear. The lamp was purchased as a Hobbs, Brockunier piece, date unknown. It is 32.5"h x 6.5"b. $550-600. *Courtesy of Bill McFarling.*

A Pairpoint vase, c. early 1900s. This very attractive double handled vase has a cut vintage pattern, 11"h x 4.25"b. $650-700.

A Pairpoint candy dish, c. early 1900s. The lip of the bowl and the lid have a cut vintage design, 6.5"h x 7"d. $600-650.

An art glass bowl, maker unknown but was purchased as Sandwich, c.1890s. This bowl with a crimped top is cased, white on the outside and blue on the inside, with canary applied edge and feet. It is 4"h x 6"d. $225-250.

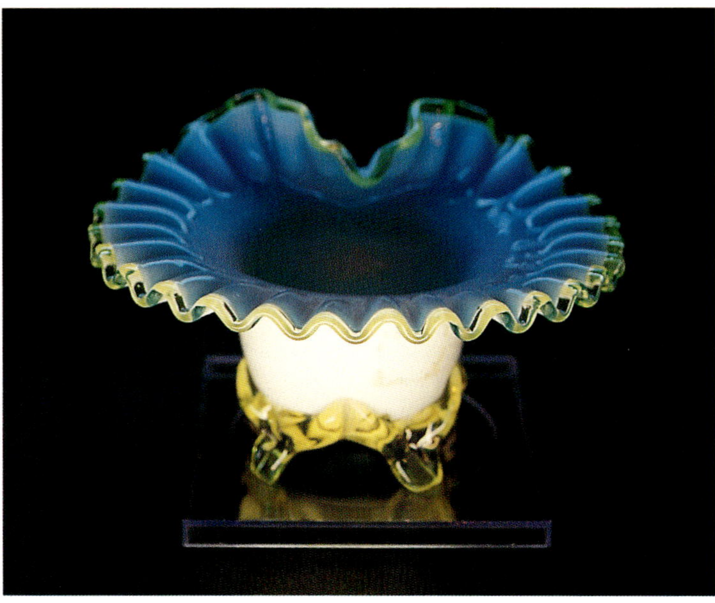

Art Glass. These three pieces were purchased as Sandwich Art Glass, c.1890s. The blown *Jack-in-Pulpit* vase in the center has a canary bottom. Its slender neck and top are faintly opalescent. The top is trimmed with cranberry. There is an applied cranberry flower and applied canary leaves, 8.5"h x 2.1"b. The two blown ewers on the sides are blue and cranberry opalescent with applied handles and leaves in canary and applied flowers in cranberry, 7.25"h x 2.6"b. $200-225 ea.

Blackberry Spray bowls. Two carnival vaseline bowls by Fenton, c.1911. These bowls are referred to as violet vases. The bowls are vaseline cased with red and marigold carnival. 2.5"h x 6"d and 3"h x 6.5"d. Two views are shown for better illustration. The vaseline is most evident around the top and bottom edges. $105-115 ea.

Carnival Vaseline bowl by Fenton, c.1915. The pattern of this 3 legged vaseline carnival bowl is *Two Flowers (Dogwood and Marsh Lily)* in Topaz, 7"d. $115-145. *Courtesy of Laura Kelm and Pete Buck.*

Carnival Vaseline bowl by Fenton, c.1911. This 6" fluted bowl is called a violet vase. The pattern is *Holly* in Topaz iridescent. $100-115. *Courtesy of Laura Kelm and Pete Buck.*

A single lily epergne, maker unknown, c.1890s. This epergne has an opalescent, ribbed, fluted lily, and an ornate metal base, 17"h x 7"b, top is 6.6"w. $325-350. *Courtesy of Bill McFarling.*

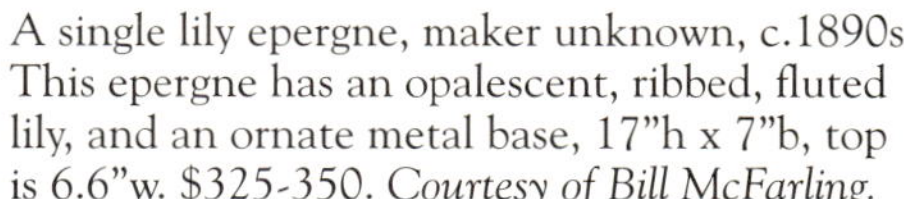

A match holder base lamp by French Potter and Wilson, c.1886. This all glass lamp has a place to hold matches on two sides of the base. On two of the vertical sides of the base there are corrugations to use as a striker. It measures 15.5"h x 4"b. The font is 5"d. $475-500.

This 19th century whale oil lamp made by Plume and Atwood Manufacturing Co. has *The P. & A. Mfg. Co. Victor* embossed on the thumbwheel. It has a round wick burner and is 17.25"h x 3.5"b. $575-650.

Left:
A lampshade, maker and date unknown. This vaseline opalescent lampshade with a cranberry trim around the top is 3.5"h x 6.25"d. $150-200. This shade is pictured on a lamp below. *Courtesy of Laura Kelm and Pete Buck.*

Left:
Whiskey jug, maker and date unknown. This jug has a fleur-de-lis emblem on the front, 6.25"h x 5"d. $75-100. *Courtesy of Laura Kelm and Pete Buck.*

A group of top hats. The hat on the left is a *Thousand Eye* toothpick, c.1888-1895. This toothpick was made by three different companies, Adams Glass, Richards and Hartley, and U. S. Glass. 2.15"h. The center hat is a *Tapered Block* toothpick by Fostoria Glass, c.1900, 2.25"h. The hat on the right is a *Daisy and Button* toothpick by U. S. Glass Factory D (Duncan and Sons), c.1892, 2.5"h. The small hat in the back is a *Daisy and Button* salt by U. S. Glass Factory D (Duncan and Sons), c.1892. $65-75 ea. *Courtesy of Laura Kelm and Pete Buck.*

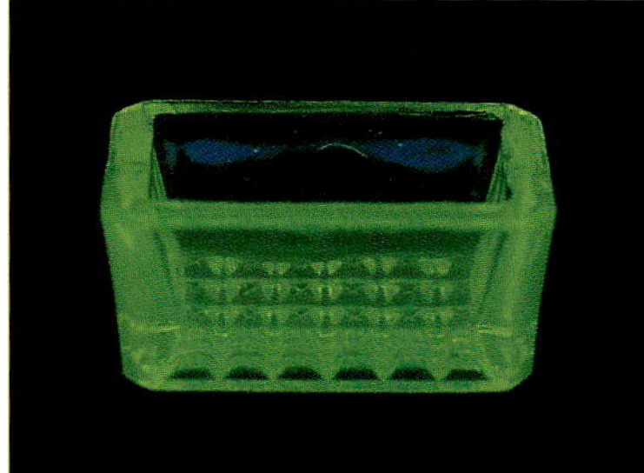

This is an early Cambridge open salt. The sides of this pressed rectangular salt are plain, the base has rows of tiny squares, .9"h x 2"l x 1.25"w. $55-65. *Courtesy of Laura Kelm and Pete Buck.*

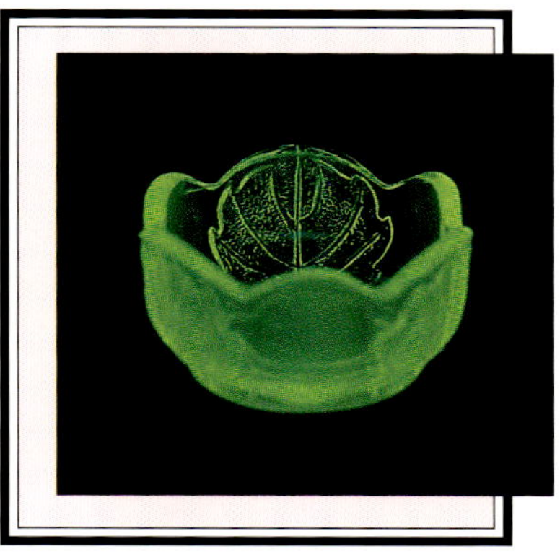

Leaf and Rib, maker unknown, c.1890. This canary open salt is 1"h. $45-50. *Courtesy of Laura Kelm and Pete Buck.*

A commemorative cup, maker unknown. This engraved 1893 World's Fair commemorative cup is 2.4"h x 2"d. $75-100. *Courtesy of Laura Kelm and Pete Buck.*

Daisy and Button skuttle by U. S. Glass Factory A (Adams and Co.), c.1891. This little coal bucket functioned both as a toothpick and a match holder, 2.5"h x 2"w. $45-48. *Courtesy of Laura Kelm and Pete Buck.*

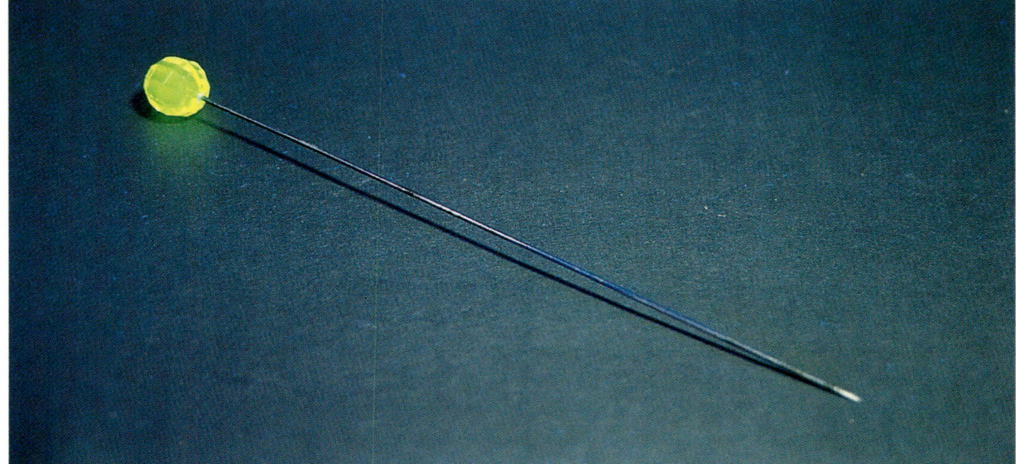

Hat pin, maker and circa unknown. This vaseline hat pin is 8.25"l. $95-115. *Courtesy of Laura Kelm and Pete Buck.*

Thousand Eye pitcher, maker and circa unknown. This little pitcher has a ribbed triangular top, and the body has a striped design, which alternates between opalescence and an iridescence. The applied handle is amber, 4.9"h x 2.7"d. $115-125. Help with identification would be appreciated.

Chapter III.
The 1920s to the 1940s

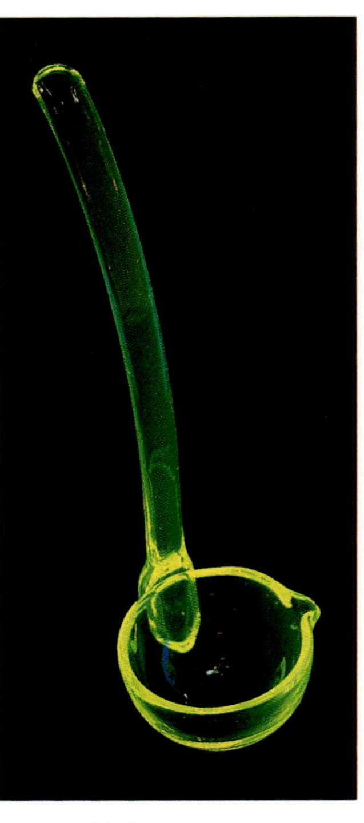

A punch set, maker unknown but possibly Fostoria or Cambridge, c.1920s. This beautiful punch set has a cut flower and leaf design. The covered punch bowl is 9.75"h x 8.25"d. The cups are 2.6"h x 3.1"d, and the ladle shown individually at right is 11.5"l. $1200-1400 set. *Courtesy of Larry and Lois Smith.*

A large fruit bowl, maker unknown, possibly c.1920s. This large bowl has 12 panels around it and is a very deep vaseline color, 5.5"h x 8.6"d. $300-350.

This is a large clear vaseline bowl by possibly Fostoria or Cambridge, c.1920s. It is 4"h x 9.5"d. $110-130. *Courtesy of Laura Kelm and Pete Buck.*

A vegetable bowl, maker unknown but possibly Fostoria, c.1920s. This bowl measures 3.25"h x 8.9"w. $60-85.

A *Stretch Glass* bowl, maker unknown, possibly Fenton, c. 1920s. This footed stretch glass bowl is 3.8"h x 7"d. $200-225. *Courtesy of Laura Kelm and Pete Buck.*

Acid etched bowl by Tiffin Glass Co., c.1930. This looped top acid etched bowl is in the Jack Frost pattern. 2.5"h x 10.75"d. $150-175. *Courtesy of Laura Kelm and Pete Buck.*

A cracker jar, maker unknown, c.1920s. This interesting jar has matching ladies on all four sides. A ribbed curtain is tied back and the ladies are kneeling each holding what appears to be a book or picture in her hand. The ladies have wavy hair, are wearing elegant low-cut gowns, and are barefooted. The sides of the jar are frosted but the ladies stand out (as if in three dimension) in clear glass. There are 2 clear glass ribs at the corners of the jar. 7.75"h x 4.75"w. $275-300. *Courtesy of Larry and Lois Smith.*

A tall compote, maker possibly Fostoria, c.1920s. This high standard open compote with twisted stem has an etched flower design and is 7"h x 7.4"d, x 3.65"b. $225-250. *Courtesy of Larry and Lois Smith.*

A mayonnaise dish and ladle, possibly Fostoria, c.1924-1927. Fostoria made canary glass from 1924 through 1927. This 4.25"h x 5.85"d bowl and 5"l ladle are representative of shapes made during this period. $110-130 and $20-25 respectively.

Sandwich plate by Cambridge, c.1920s. This double handled, octagonal, opalescent sandwich plate is 10.5"d. $125-150.

Sandwich plate by Fostoria, c.1924-1927. This center handled sandwich is one of Fostoria's optic, cut patterns. Notice the flower design with vertical ribs, 11.5"d. $125-150. *Courtesy of Laura Kelm and Pete Buck.*

A covered nut dish by Fostoria, c.1924-1927. This is a piece of Fostoria's optic, cut ware with a flower design measuring 5.25"h x 6.75"d. $200-225.

This is another example of Fostoria's nut dish. It is like photo shown at left but without the design. $150-175. *Courtesy of Larry and Lois Smith.*

A Fostoria candy jar, c.1924-1927. This typical candy jar has white trim on the edge of the lid and on the base and top edge of the bowl, 3.5"h x 5"d. $150-200.

Candy dish, maker unknown, c.1920s. This 3 legged candy dish has a lot of green color to it. It is 5"h x 5.75"d. $125-150.

Candy dish, maker unknown, possibly c.1930s. This candy dish has a clear bowl and base and a vaseline lid, 7"h x 5"d. $95-125.

Plate, sherbet, and cup by Fostoria, c.1924-1927. This plate and sherbet set is called a *Jah Jongy* set. The plate is 8.75"d. $40-45. The sherbet is 3.5"h x 3.25"d. $60-65. The cup is 2.25"h x 3.5"d. $28-30. *Courtesy of Laura Kelm and Pete Buck.*

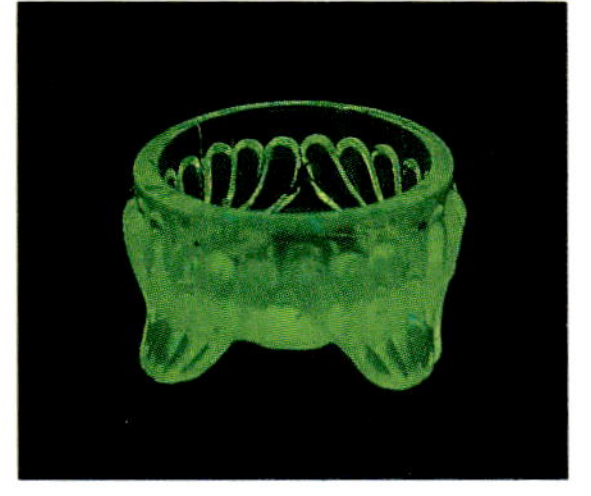

Cambridge's *Caprice* almond cups open salt, c.1920s. This four footed salt was reproduced by Imperial Glass in the seventies. 1"h, $35-45. *Courtesy of Laura Kelm and Pete Buck.*

Crackle glass sherbets by L. E. Smith, c.1926. This pattern is known as *"By Cracky."* 3"h x 2.4"b. $50-75 ea.

A water pitcher with a paneled pattern, maker unknown, c.1930s. This is a half-gallon pitcher and is 8"h. $325-350.

Compote by Westmoreland, c.1920s. This double handled banana dish resembles the Colonial pattern, 6.25"l x 3.25"w x 3.75"h. $75-110.

Paneled pitcher, maker unknown, c.1920s-30s. This small pitcher is 4.75"h. $125-150. *Courtesy of Laura Kelm and Pete Buck.*

A fan vase by Fenton, c.1937. This fan vase is in Fenton's *Cape Cod* design, 9.5"h x 9"w x 4.5"b. $150-175. *Courtesy of Larry and Lois Smith.*

Decanter and shot glasses, maker possibly Cambridge, c.1920s. The decanter is 10"h. $225-250. The shot glasses have an etched flower design and are 2.25"h x 1.75'd. $25-30 ea. *Courtesy of Laura Kelm and Pete Buck.*

Perfume bottle. The maker of this 1920s perfume bottle with an encrusted gold flower design is unknown but possibly Fostoria. $225-250. *Courtesy of Melanie Schonier.*

"Milady" vanity set by Tiffin Glass, c.1930s. The two perfume bottles with the turban shaped stoppers are slightly different. The swirl pattern is more distinct on the body of the shorter one. They measure 3.75"h and 3.5"h x 1.6"d. The puff box has the swirl pattern on the inside of the lid, 3.5"h x 3.75"d. $140-160 ea.

Perfume bottle by Cambridge, c. late 1920s. This perfume with hand painted flowers measures 4.7"h. $150-175.

Left:
Perfumes by Tiffin, c.1920-1930s. Two sizes of Tiffin perfumes with large discs at the top of the bodies and tapered stems. One has a mushroom type stopper. The larger perfume without a stopper is 5.5"h, $85-95. The other perfume is 6"h, $175-200. *Courtesy of Laura Kelm and Pete Buck.*

Opalescent perfume bottles. The perfume on the right resembles a DeVilbiss bottle but was made for a company in Chartley, Mass., and marketed as *"Holm Spray"* in the 1940s. Not original stopper. $125-150. The *Petticoats* atomizer on the left was made by Fenton for DeVilbiss Company, c.1933. The atomizer is missing. It is 4.25"h x 2.75"d. $125-150. *Courtesy of Laura Kelm and Pete Buck.*

Fostoria powder, c.1924-1927. This powder or vanity set is unusual in that it has the perfume bottle as the handle of the powder box lid. The lid of this powder has etched flowers, 7"h x 4.5"d. $325-350.

Fostoria powder. See description of powder, above. This powder has no design. $300-325. *Courtesy of Laura Kelm and Pete Buck.*

A perfume bottle by Tiffin, c.1920-1930s. This 7"h perfume has its dauber. It is very hard to find perfumes with daubers as they broke quite easily during use. $275-300. *Courtesy of Larry and Lois Smith.*

A cologne, maker unknown, c.1930s. The design of this square cologne is alternating buttons and Xs. It is 5.5"h x 1.8"sq. $225-250. *Courtesy of Laura Kelm and Pete Buck.*

A cologne, maker unknown, c.1930s. This cologne with a large stopper has a diamond type pattern and is 5.5d"h x 1.75"d. $250-275. *Courtesy of Laura Kelm and Pete Buck.*

Decanter, maker unknown, c.1930s. This decanter has a diamond pattern around the center. Stopper missing, 5.5"h x 2.75"d. $120-140. *Courtesy of Laura Kelm and Pete Buck.*

Candleholders, maker unknown, c. 1920s. This pretty pair of candleholders can be inverted and used as vases. 9"h x 4.75"b. $195-225.

A pair of candleholders, maker unknown, c.1920s. These twisted satin glass candleholders are 8"h x 4"b. $175-200.

Candleholders, maker and circa unknown. These candleholders have clear bases and are 10.5"h. $140-160. *Courtesy of Laura Kelm and Pete Buck.*

A pair of *Twisted Optic* candleholders by Imperial, c.1920s. 3.5"h x 3.4"b. $50-75 ea.

Candleholders, maker possibly Cambridge, c. late 1920s - early 1930s. This pair of short candleholders measure 3"h x 4.85"b. $150-175 pr. *Courtesy of Laura Kelm and Pete Buck.*

A car vase, maker unknown, c.1927. This flared and fluted top car vase with a flower design is 6.75"h x 4.5"d. $175-200. *Courtesy of Laura Kelm and Pete Buck.*

Car vase, maker unknown, c.1929. This automobile bud vase has a flower design and is 6.25"l x 2.1"d. $125-150. *Courtesy of Laura Kelm and Pete Buck.*

A bud vase maker unknown, c.1920s. This vaseline bud vase with a cobalt base is 8.25"h x 3.1"b. $100-125.

Satin bud vase, possibly by Cambridge, c.1920-1930s. This tall cone shaped satin finish vase has a cobalt base, 10.75"h x 2.75"b. $125-150. *Courtesy of Laura Kelm and Pete Buck.*

A bud vase, maker unknown, possibly Fostoria, c. 1920s. This flared bud vase with an etched flower design is 10"h. $65-85. *Courtesy of Laura Kelm and Pete Buck.*

A *Tut* vase by Fostoria, c.1924-1928. This vase is also called a "Loving Cup". 8.25"h x 3"b. $160-200.

Whiskey glasses, maker unknown, c.1930s. These glasses are advertising pieces for Seagram. They read Seagram's Rye Whisky on the side, 3.4"h x 1.25"d. $40-50 ea. *Courtesy of Bill McFarling.*

A paneled goblet, maker unknown, c.1920s. This 6 oz. ribbed goblet is 6"h. $75-95.

Goblets, maker possibly Cambridge, c. late 1920s to early 1930s. These vaseline goblets have light purple stems and bases, 6.25"h x 2.75"sq base. $85-95 ea. *Courtesy of Laura Kelm and Pete Buck.*

A shot glass, maker unknown, c.1930s. The shot glass measures 2.75"h. $40-50. *Courtesy of Laura Kelm and Pete Buck.*

Champagne stems, maker unknown, c.1920s. The bases of these vaseline paneled champagne glasses are green, but they are fluorescing under the black-light so the color isn't evident, 5.5"h. $45-50 ea. *Courtesy of Laura Kelm and Pete Buck.*

Stems, maker unknown, c. late 1920s. This 5.25"h. goblet and two 3"h glasses are footed with green bases and a ribbed pattern. $45-50 ea. *Courtesy of Laura Kelm and Pete Buck.*

Stems, maker unknown, c.1920s. The wine glass on the left with a vaseline bowl and clear stem is 5.75"h. The champagne on the right with a blue bowl and stem and vaseline base is 5"h. $40-50 ea. *Courtesy of Laura Kelm and Pete Buck.*

Stems, maker unknown, c.1920s. A matching 4.5"h. goblet and 3.75"h. sherbet with etching around the tops and green bases. $50-60 ea. *Courtesy of Laura Kelm and Pete Buck.*

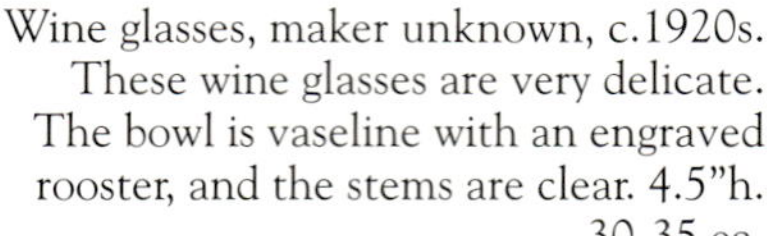

Wine glasses, maker unknown, c.1920s. These wine glasses are very delicate. The bowl is vaseline with an engraved rooster, and the stems are clear. 4.5"h. 30-35 ea.

A handled Lemon Slice server by Fenton, c.1926. This Topaz iridescent handled lemon slice server is 2"h x 4.5"d. $45-50. *Courtesy of Laura Kelm and Pete Buck.*

A *Hobnail* cruet. The maker and date of this hobnail cruet are unknown. Not original stopper, $125-175. *Courtesy of Melanie Schonier.*

Turkey Tracks bowl possibly by Steuben, c.1925-1930. This bowl has an amber color in the natural light, but glows nicely under black light. 2.8"h x 5.3"d. $50-75.

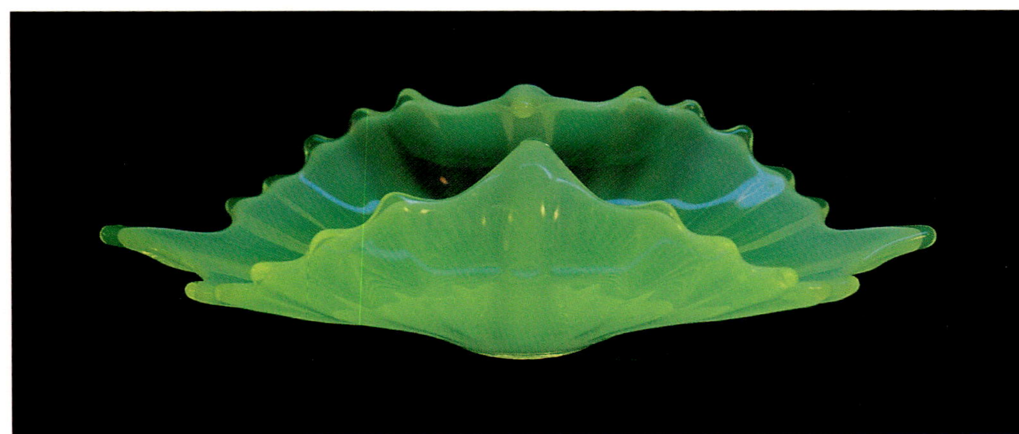

A *Heirloom* basket by Fostoria, c.1959-1970, 10.25"l x 5.15"w. $150-175.

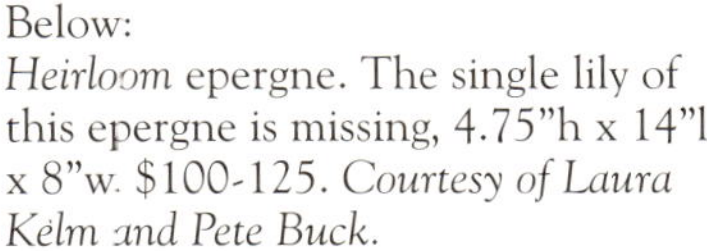

Below:
Heirloom epergne. The single lily of this epergne is missing, 4.75"h x 14"l x 8"w. $100-125. *Courtesy of Laura Kelm and Pete Buck.*

Heirloom star plate,
10"d. $75-100.
*Courtesy of Laura
Kelm and Pete Buck.*

Heirloom bowl, 4.5"h x 5.75"d. $75-95.
Courtesy of Laura Kelm and Pete Buck.

Twiggy dish. This leaf design dish was
made by Indiana Glass, c.1920s, 6.25"l
x 6.25"w. $55-75.

Fenton leaf #175, c.1940s. This
opalescent leaf was made in two sizes.
This is the 11" cake plate. $100-125.

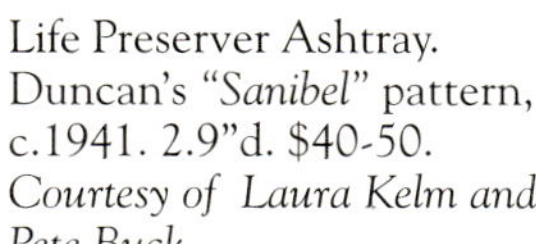

Life Preserver Ashtray.
Duncan's *"Sanibel"* pattern,
c.1941. 2.9"d. $40-50.
*Courtesy of Laura Kelm and
Pete Buck.*

A *Sanibel* nappy. This shell
shaped fruit nappy has very
heavy opalescence, 6.5"l x
5.5"d. $75-95.

A boudoir lamp by Fostoria, c.1920s. This
is one of Fostoria's optic, cut patterns.
The base has a scalloped bottom, and the
design consists of vertical ribs and
flowers. The shade has an etched leaf
design. Two of the original vaseline
teardrop prisms are missing. The lamp
measures 14"h x 5"b. $475-500.

Daisy and Fern oil lamp by Fenton, c.1930s. This pretty oil lamp has a clear crystal base, 19.25"h x 5.75"b. $425-475. *Courtesy of Laura Kelm and Pete Buck.*

An electric lamp, maker unknown, c.1930s. This opalescent, striped lamp has a metal base and is 19"h x 5.5"b. $325-350.

A *Daisy and Fern* oil lamp possibly by Fenton, c.1930s. This *Daisy and Fern* lamp with a milk glass base is 18.75"h x 5.15"b. $475-525.

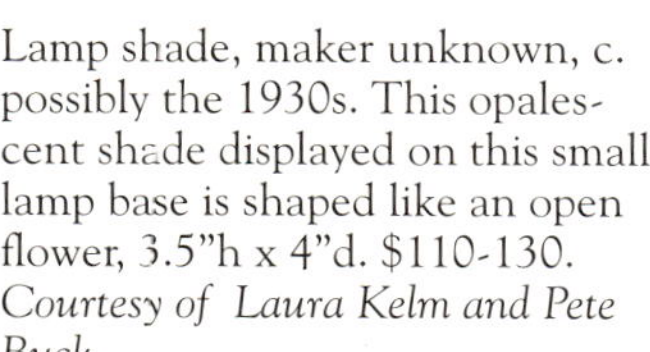

Lamp shade, maker unknown, c. possibly the 1930s. This opalescent shade displayed on this small lamp base is shaped like an open flower, 3.5"h x 4"d. $110-130. *Courtesy of Laura Kelm and Pete Buck.*

Barber bottle, maker and circa unknown. This opalescent, coin spot design, rolled lip barber bottle is 10"h. $150-175. *Courtesy of Laura Kelm and Pete Buck.*

A candy dish by Cambridge, c.1920-1930s. This clover shaped candy dish is 4"h x 8"w. $150-165.

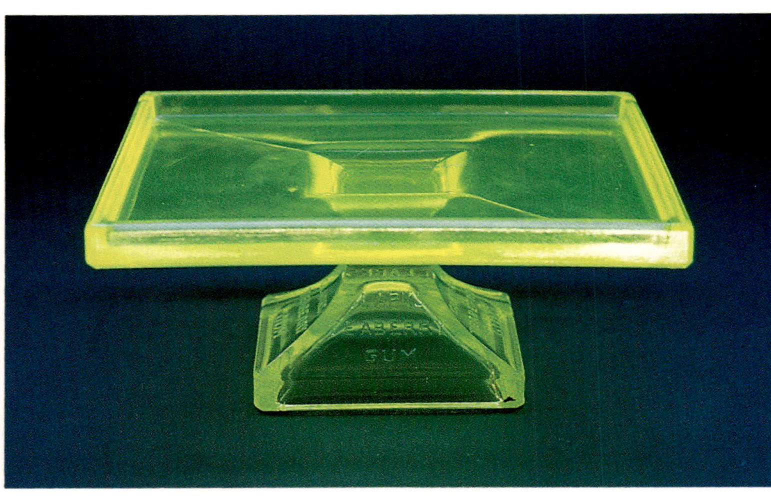

Clarks Teaberry Gum Stand, c.1928. This stand was used as an advertising piece in stores during this period to display Clarks gum. 3.25"h x 6.75"l x 4.75"w. $130-185.

Honey jar, c. unknown. Top is James W. Tufts silver-plate. The domed top looks like a beehive with bees and flowers engraved around the base. 5" h x 4.85"sq. $275-300.

Compote with gold overlay featuring woman seated in Grecian garden holding a garland of flowers, c.1930s. 5.5"h x 4.85"d. $125-150.

A cigarette lighter, maker unknown, c.1930s. The lighter part has "Evans USA" on the bottom. The design on the glass part of the stand consists of 3 rows of English type hobnail and 2 rows of solid bars. These columns are swirled. 3.5"h x 2.5"d. $125-150. *Courtesy of Laura Kelm and Pete Buck.*

Hobnail cigarette set by Fenton, c.1941-1943. The large hat used for cigarettes is 2.5"h. The little hat used for matches is 1.5"h. And, the round ash tray is 2.75"d. $175-200 set. *Courtesy of Laura Kelm and Pete Buck.*

Hand vase by Fenton, c.1941-1943. This Topaz hand vase is 3.5"h. It has been reproduced. $75-85. *Courtesy of Laura Kelm and Pete Buck.*

Hobnail vanity set by Fenton, c.1941-1943. The perfumes of this 3 piece Hobnail vanity set are 4.5"h x 2.25"d. The powder box is 2.75"h x 3.5"d. $90-100 ea. *Courtesy of Laura Kelm and Pete Buck.*

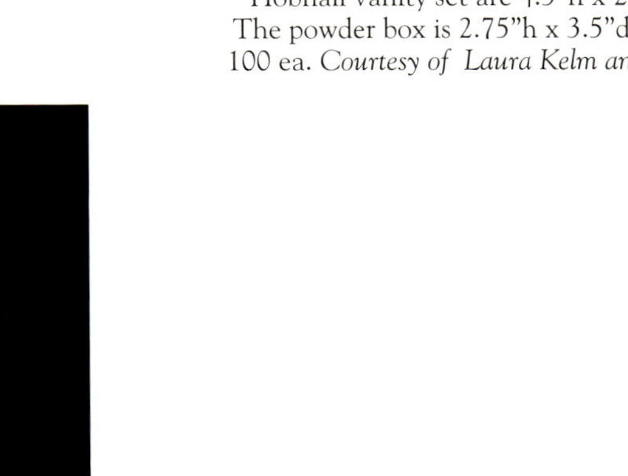

Hobnail candlesticks by Fenton, c.1941-1943. This pair of Hobnail candlesticks is 3.5"h x 4.25"b. $225-250 pr. *Courtesy of Laura Kelm and Pete Buck.*

A *Hobnail* candy jar by Fenton, c.1941-1943. This footed, covered candy jar is 7"h x 4.7"d x 5"b. $110-125.

A *Hobnail* basket by Fenton, c.1941-1943. This is the large 7" Fenton basket. $175-200. *Courtesy of Laura Kelm and Pete Buck.*

Fenton *Hobnail* basket, c.1941-1943. Notice the difference in the shape of this 7" basket and the basket at left. $175-200. *Courtesy of Laura Kelm and Pete Buck.*

Hobnail creamers and sugars by Fenton, c.1941-1943. The creamer and sugar on the front row are 3.5"h. $45-50 ea. The individual creamer and sugar on the back row are 2"h. $30-35 ea. *Courtesy of Laura Kelm and Pete Buck.*

A group of *Hobnail* vases by Fenton, c.1941-1943. Left to right, a mini-cornucopia candlestick or vase, a Crimped vase, a Triangle vase, a Fan vase. All are 4"h, $65-75 ea. *Courtesy of Laura Kelm and Pete Buck.*

Fenton *Hobnail* bowls, c.1941-1943. The square top bowl on the left is 3.5"h and the crimped top rose bowl on the right is 4.5"h. $125-135 ea. *Courtesy of Laura Kelm and Pete Buck.*

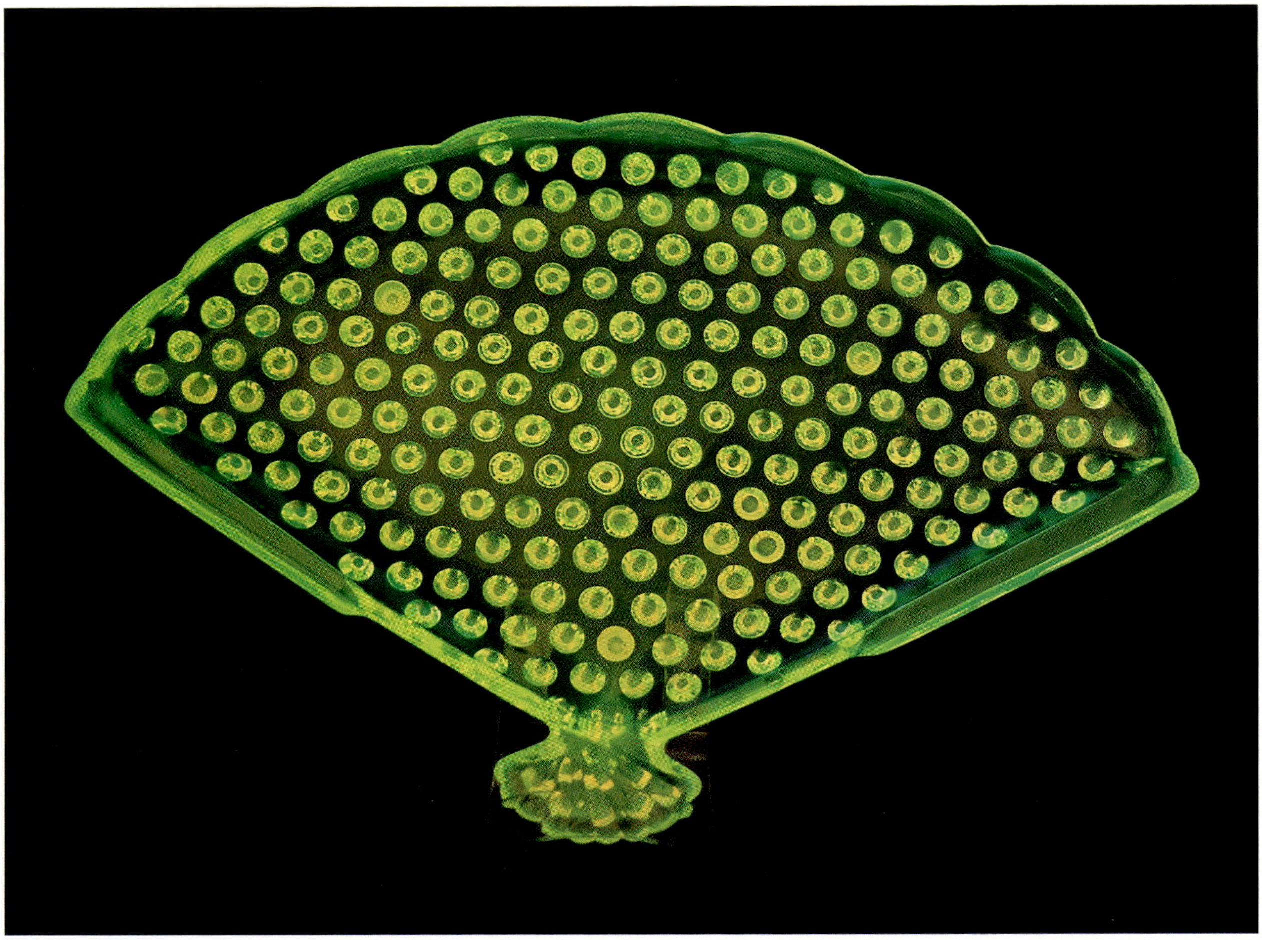

A Fenton *Hobnail* fan, c.1941-1943. This 10.5" fan can be used as a relish tray or as part of a vanity set. $100-125. *Courtesy of Laura Kelm and Pete Buck.*

Hobnail vases by Fenton, c.1941-1943. The triangle vase on the left is 4"h, and the flared vase on the right is 5.5"h. $80-100 ea. *Courtesy of Laura Kelm and Pete Buck.*

Hobnail compote by Fenton c. 1941-1943. The catalog refers to this compote as a double crimped 12" footed bowl. $200-225. *Courtesy of Laura Kelm and Pete Buck.*

Hobnail cake plate by Fenton, c.1941-1943. This footed cake plate is 5"h x 12"d. $250-300. *Courtesy of Laura Kelm and Pete Buck.*

Fenton *Hobnail* bowl, c.1941-1943. This *Hobnail* double crimped bonbon dish is 6"d. $100-115. *Courtesy of Laura Kelm and Pete Buck.*

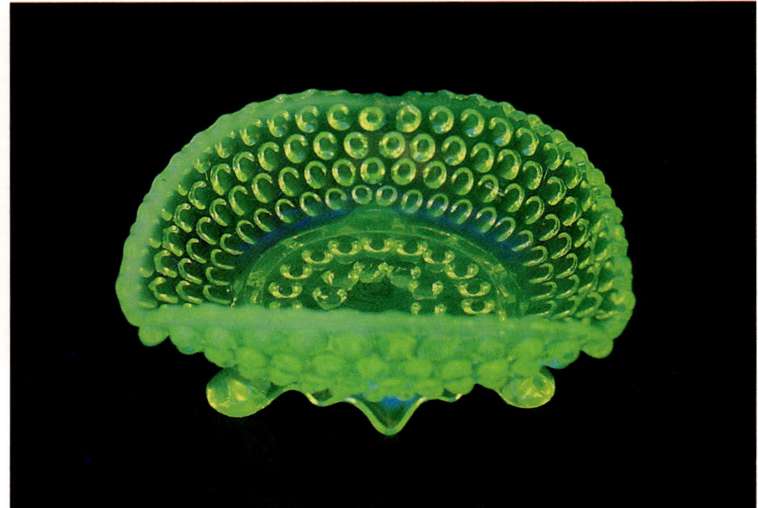

Hobnail nappy, maker unknown. This triangle shape opalescent hobnail nappy has 3 feet. $65-75. *Courtesy of Laura Kelm and Pete Buck.*

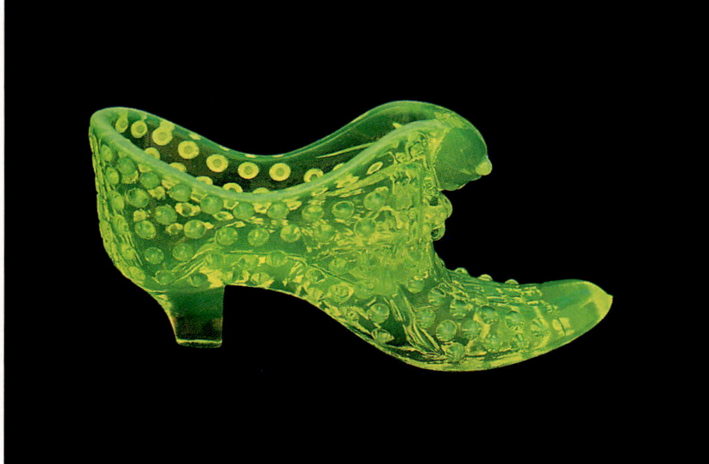

Fenton *Hobnail* slipper, c.1941-1943. This slipper has a cat's head on the front and is 6"l. $55-65. *Courtesy of Laura Kelm and Pete Buck.*

Hobnail basket. This is Fenton's 7" handled basket in *Hobnail*, c.1941-1943. $100-125. *Courtesy of Laura Kelm and Pete Buck.*

A *Hobnail* tumbler by Fenton, c.1948.
This 4 oz. tumbler is Fenton's Topaz.
$30-50.

A *Hobnail* pitcher by Fenton, c.1941-
1943. This little Topaz pitcher is 5.5"h
x 2.2"b. $150-175.

A *Daisy and Button* fan by Fenton, c.1937. This piece was advertised to be used as a bon bon,
dresser tray, salad plate, or hors d'oeuvre tray, 10.5"l x 7"w. $75-100.

A *Wreathed Cherry* creamer. This pattern was originally produced by Dungan, c.1908. It was reproduced by L. G. Wright, c.1968-1970. The design on this pitcher is very defined, however I am not sure if it is an original. $85-95.

A *Dolphin* compote by Westmoreland for L. G. Wright, c.1950-60s. This is a reproduction. The dolphin stem is solid. It is 5.5"h x 6.25"d. $70-85. *Courtesy of Laura Kelm and Pete Buck.*

A *Hobnail* finger bowl, maker and circa unknown. This footed Hobnail finger bowl has a scalloped top and a thumbprint pattern on the base, 3.1"h x 4.25"d. $175-200. *Courtesy of Laura Kelm and Pete Buck.*

Jersey Swirl goblets by L. G. Wright,
c.late 1950s to early 1960s. $50-55 ea.
Courtesy of Laura Kelm and Pete Buck.

A plain butter dish, maker unknown,
possibly c.1950s. This paneled butter
dish is 5"h x 7.5"d. $250-275.

A hobnail butter dish, maker unknown,
possibly c.1950s. This 5 footed hobnail
butter dish is 4.75"h x 7"d. $250-275.

A *Moon and Stars* decanter and wine glasses made by Fenton for L. G. Wright. The opalescent decanter is c.1976 and is 12"h x 5.75"d. $400-$450. These 4 oz. opalescent wine glasses are c.1960s and are 4.5"h. $65-75 ea.

A *Moon and Stars* goblet made by Fenton for L. G. Wright, c.1960s. This 8 oz. opalescent goblet is 5.75"h. $85-95.

Daisy and Button basket by L. G. Wright, c.1960s. The pattern on this tall basket is not well defined, 7.5"h x 2.75"b. $95-110.

Thousand Eye goblet by Westmoreland c.1950s. This 8 oz. goblet is 6"h. $75-95.

Panel Grape goblets made by Westmoreland for L. G. Wright, c.1968. These are 6"h, 6 oz. opalescent goblets. $75-95 ea.

Strawberry and Currant goblets by Fenton for L. G. Wright, c.1971. One of these opalescent goblets shows the strawberry design, and the other shows the currant design. They are 8 oz. and measure 6.25"h. $75-95 ea.

A *Daisy and Button* sugar by L. G. Wright, c.1960s. This opalescent *Daisy and Button* sugar is 3.4"h x 1.9"b. $48-65.

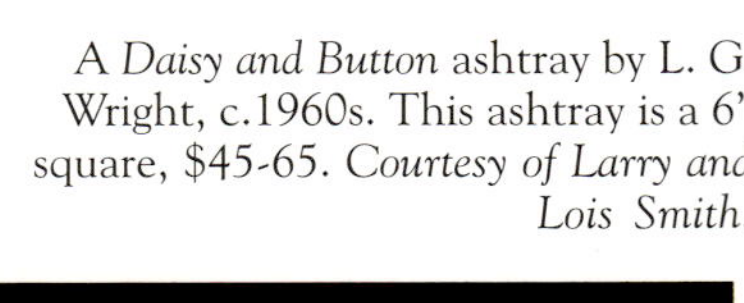

A *Daisy and Button* ashtray by L. G. Wright, c.1960s. This ashtray is a 6" square, $45-65. *Courtesy of Larry and Lois Smith.*

Daisy and Button with Thumbprint, L. G. Wright, c.1960s. These 8 oz. opalescent goblets are 6"h x 3.2"d and were made by Fenton for Wright. $75-100 ea.

Daisy and Button with Thumbprint wine glasses by Fenton for L. G. Wright, c.1960s. These 4 oz. opalescent wine glasses measure 4.75"h x 2.5"d. $70-75 ea.

Daisy and Button with Thumbprint compote by L. G. Wright, c.1930s. This covered high standard compote is 9.25"h x 5.75"sq. $250-325.

Opalescent candleholders made by Fenton for L. G. Wright, c.1960s. These are reproductions of the Northwood *Opal Open* pattern of 1910. The loops on the base are solid. 5"h x 3.3"b. $60-95 ea.

A large *Opal Open* crimped bowl made by Fenton for L. G. Wright, c.1960s. This bowl was sometimes combined with candleholders, shown above, and used as a console set. 6.5"h x 4"b. $110-145.

Atlantis vase by Fenton, c.1997. This vase has an iridescent finish and is 6.75"h x 5.75"d. $75-100. *Courtesy of Laura Kelm and Pete Buck.*

Tulip vase by Fenton, c. late 1990s. This *Fine Dot* tulip vase measures 11"h x 4.3"b. $95-110.

Tulip vase by Fenton, c.1997. This *Daisy and Fern* tulip vase is trimmed in cobalt, 11.5"h x 4.25"b. $75-100. *Courtesy of Laura Kelm and Pete Buck.*

Above:
Jack-in-Pulpit vase by Fenton, c.1990s. This opalescent reverse swirl vase is 7.75"h x 5.25"d. $125-150. *Courtesy of Laura Kelm and Pete Buck.*

Far left:
Lily-of-the-Valley vase by Fenton, c.1980s. This vase is referred to as a handkerchief vase, 6.5"h x 4.5"d. $85-100. *Courtesy of Laura Kelm and Pete Buck.*

Left:
Lily-of-the-Valley fairy light by Fenton, c.1980s. 7"h x 3.1"b. $130-150.

ABC plate, maker and circa unknown. This ABC plate is marked Clay's Crystal Works on the back, 8"d. $50-75. *Courtesy of Laura Kelm and Pete Buck.*

A powder jar by Imperial Glass, c.1965. This *Dew Drop* powder jar has the Imperial Glass logo in the bottom. $140-160.

An Ivy Bowl by Imperial Glass, c.1965. This *Dew Drop* ivy bowl, marked with the Imperial Glass logo "I" with "G" on top, is 6.5"h x 3.5"d. $55-75. *Courtesy of Laura Kelm and Pete Buck.*

Drapery bowl, 4"h x 5.25"d. $100-125.

A *Drapery* basket by Fenton, c.1988. This footed basket has a ribbon candy edge. The Fenton logo is very small. 8"h x 8"d. $145-175.

Hobnail bud vases by Fenton, c.1960s. The vases measure 8.75"h x 2.5"b. $50-75 ea. *Courtesy of Laura Kelm and Pete Buck.*

Daisy and Fern pitcher made by Fenton for L. G. Wright in the mid-1960s. This pitcher was made in 3 different shapes. Notice the difference in the shape of the top of this pitcher compared to the one seen on the next page, center left, 9"h. $275-295. *Courtesy of Laura Kelm and Pete Buck.*

Daisy and Fern tea glasses. These 10 oz. ice teas are 5.15"h x 2.75"d. $50-60. *Courtesy of Laura Kelm and Pete Buck.*

A *Daisy and Fern* water set made by Fenton for L. G. Wright. The tumblers are c.1960s, 3.7"h x 2.9"d. $65-75. This pitcher is c.1976. Compare to photo 304. $225-250.

A *Daisy and Fern* barber bottle made by Fenton for L. G. Wright, c.1960s. This bottle is 8.25"h x 2.5"b. $165-185.

A *Daisy and Fern* syrup pitcher made by Fenton for L. G. Wright, c.1979. This syrup pitcher measures 6.5"h x 2.9"b. $145-165.

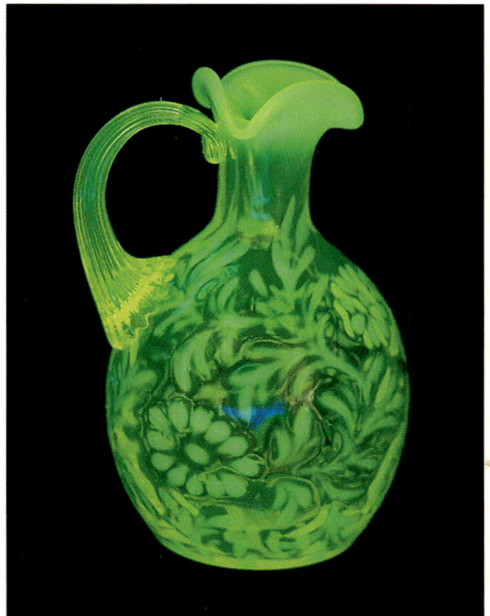

Daisy and Fern cruet made by Fenton
for L. G. Wright, c.1960s. This cruet
with missing stopper is 5.5"h.
$150-175. *Courtesy of Laura Kelm and
Pete Buck.*

Daisy and Fern vase by Fenton, c.1997.
This large, 11"h x 8.5"d, vase is
Fenton's *Fern* pattern. $175-225.
Courtesy of Laura Kelm and Pete Buck.

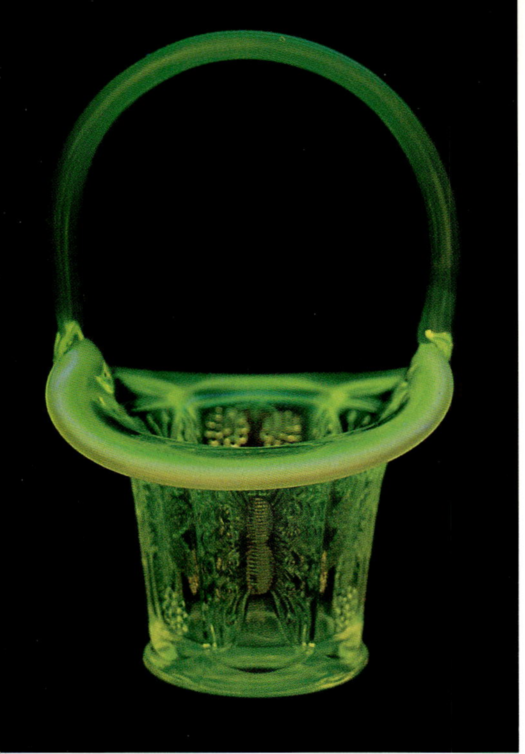

A Fenton basket c.1980s. This is a 5"
Butterfly and Berry basket. $95-125.
Courtesy of Laura Kelm and Pete Buck.

Epergne by Fenton, c.1997. This opalescent four lily epergne has an iridized finish. $300-350. *Courtesy of Laura Kelm and Pete Buck.*

Hobnail water set made for Levay by Fenton, c.1983. The pitcher is 8"h x 3.5"b; the tumbler is 4.2"h x 3"d. $325-375 set. *Courtesy of Laura Kelm and Pete Buck.*

Hobnail banana stand made for Levay by Fenton, c.1980. This pie crust crimped banana stand is marked with the Fenton logo, 6"h x 12"l x 8.75"w. $150-175. *Courtesy of Laura Kelm and Pete Buck.*

Hobnail butter and toothpick made by Fenton for Levay, c.1980. These pieces are marked with the Fenton logo. The covered butter is 4.75"h x 8.25"d, $150-175, and the toothpick is 2.75"h x 2.15"d. $30-40. *Courtesy of Laura Kelm and Pete Buck.*

Hobnail pieces by Fenton. The 3.75"h, footed salt and pepper, c. 1980s are signed with the Fenton logo. $85-95 pair. The 2"h individual creamer, c.1950s is not signed. $20-25

A *Hobnail* basket with cobalt handle by Fenton. The Fenton logo on this 6.25"h x 4.5"d basket is very small. The Handler's mark is Delmer Stowasser, 1980-1990s. $85-110.

A Fenton basket, c.1990s. This 7" hand-painted basket is signed by D. Fredrick. $75-100. *Courtesy of Larry and Lois Smith.*

A *Hobnail* basket by Fenton, c.1953-1954. This basket has a clear handle and is 6.5"h x 5"d. $95-125.

A *Hobnail* basket by Fenton. This basket is iridescent and where the vaseline handle attaches to the basket, the Handler's mark is Junior Thompson's, 1990-1993. The basket measures 6"h x 4.4"d. $75-100.

Hydrangea fairy lights by Fenton, c.1997. Notice the difference in the shape of the tops of these 7"h lights. $125-135ea. *Courtesy of Laura Kelm and Pete Buck.*

A cruet by Fenton, c.1980s. This *Coin Dot* pattern cruet is 6.75"h x 3.85"d. $135-145.

A Fenton *Hobnail* slipper, c.1990s. This hand painted and signed Hobnail slipper is 2.5"h x 5.75"l. $40-50. *Courtesy of Laura Kelm and Pete Buck.*

Vaseline shoes by Fenton and Mosser, c.1990s. The Fenton iridescent flower design slipper is 2.5"h x 6"l. $20-25. The large Mosser Rose slipper is 3"h x 5.75"l. $15-18. The small Mosser Bow slipper is 2.25"h x 4.65"l. $10-15.

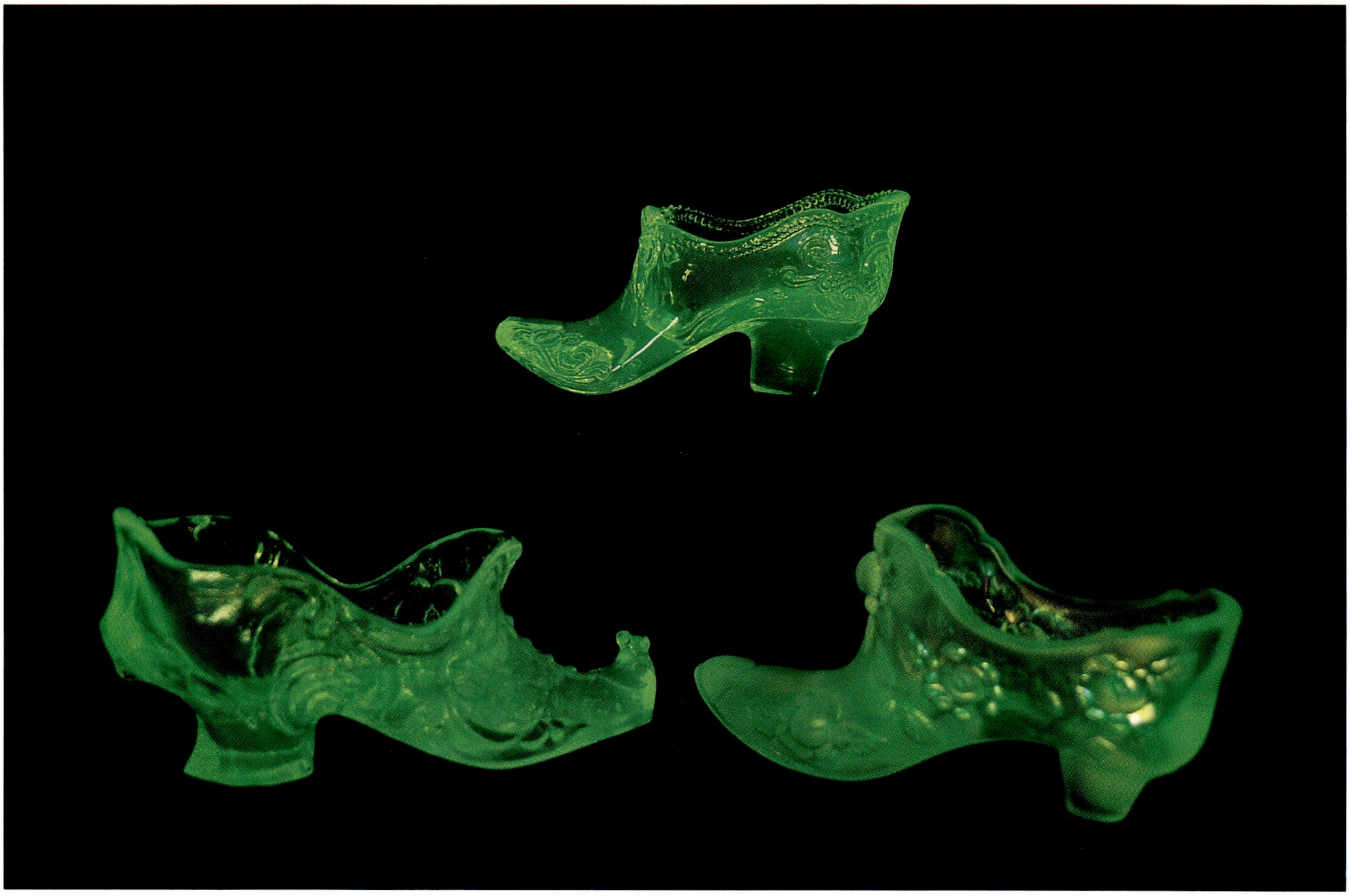

A biscuit jar, creamer, and open sugar by Westmoreland, c.1960s. This pattern is called *Plantation*. The leaves and cherries are hand painted in gold and red. The pattern is very similar to *Wreath and Cherry*. Biscuit jar is 8"h X 6.25"d. $250-275. Creamer is 3.3"h x 2.8"d. and sugar is 3.2"h x 2.9"d. $75-100 ea.

A group of opalescent Fenton animals made for Rosso, c.1998. Bear, 4"l; Cat, 3.5"l; Mouse, 2.5"h; Snail, 2.75"h x 4.25"l; Owl, 3"h; Bird, 2.75"h. $28-38. *Courtesy of Laura Kelm and Pete Buck.*

This 5.5"d plate has a picture of Mt. St. Helens in the center and the inscription "Mt. St. Helens" and "Washington" around the edge. Dated May 18, 1980. $40-50. *Courtesy of Laura Kelm and Pete Buck.*

Fairy lights. The maker and circa of these fairy lights are unknown. The frosted pineapple light is 6"h and the *Thousand Eye* one is 6.25"h. $65-75 ea. *Courtesy of Laura Kelm and Pete Buck.*

Fairy lights. The *Daisy and Button* 6"h fairy light is from the 1960s, maker unknown. $60-70. The miniature 3.5"h fairy light has a diamond pattern and is marked with Mosser's logo. $45-55. *Courtesy of Laura Kelm and Pete Buck.*

Holly pattern fairy light, maker unknown, c.1960s. This handled, footed fairy light is 5.25"h x 2.85"d. $40-50. *Courtesy of Laura Kelm and Pete Buck.*

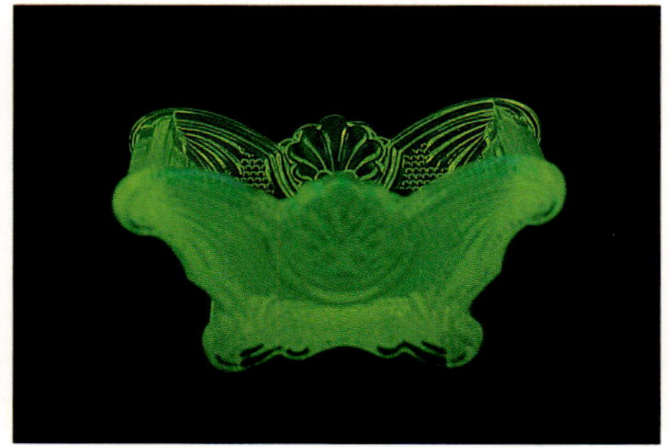

This is a Sandwich pattern salt that was reproduced for the Metropolitan Museum of Art in the1980s. It is marked "MMA", 1.75"h x 3.25"l x 1.75"w. $50-55. *Courtesy of Laura Kelm and Pete Buck.*

Daisy and Button boat made for the Metropolitan Museum of Art, c.1970s-1980s. It is marked "MMA", and is 1"h x 4.5"l x 1.75"w. $75-95. *Courtesy of Laura Kelm and Pete Buck.*

The Boyd Art Glass Company is a family business, which presently produces collectible, affordable novelties. The Boyds worked for Elizabeth Degenhart and purchased the Degenhart factory after her death in 1978. All of Boyd's glass is pressed by hand. The collector can date Boyd glass by the Diamond B logo. Every five years the logo changes: 1978-1983 B inside diamond; 1983-1988 B inside diamond with horizontal line underneath; 1988-1993 B inside diamond with horizontal line above and below; 1993-1998 B inside diamond with horizontal line above and below and a vertical line on the right. Boyd glass is unique in that many of its molds are named for family members or close friends. Boyd originally called its vaseline colored glass Firefly in 1980. In 1988 they issued the color using the names Vaseline and Vaseline carnival.

Boyd Art Glass: The train, called the *Boyd Special*, is Boyd's vaseline carnival and was made 6/17/91. The engine is 3.6"l, the coal tender is 3"l, the boxcar is 3"l, the coal hopper is 3"l, the tank car is 3"l, and the caboose is 2.5"l. $85-100. The *Boyd Airplane* made 9/10/92 is 4"l. $35-40. The *Boyd Tractor* made 5/17/91 is 2.7"l. $35-40. The *Boyd Taxi* made 5/4/94 is 3.2"l. $30-35. *Courtesy of Ben Curtis.*

Boyd Art Glass: *Chuckles,* on the left, is 4"h and was made 4/5/88. $45-50. Two views are shown of *Virgil,* since he is reversible, notice his happy and sad face. He was made 5/5/94, 4.25"h. $35-40. *Freddie Hobo Clown* on the right was made 5/28/91, 3"h. $40-50. *Courtesy of Ben Curtis.*

Boyd Art Glass: Front row left to right: *Candy Carousel Horse,* made 4/21/94, is 2"h x 1.5"l. $20-25. *Little Joe,* made 3/29/88, 2"h x 1.5"l. $20-22. *Little Luck Unicorn,* made 3/31/88, 2"h x 2"l. $18-20. Back row left to right: *Taffy Carousel Horse,* made 7/17/96, 3.75"h x 3"l. $30-32. *Joey Horse,* made 8/18/80, 3.7"h x 3"l. $35-40. *Lucky Unicorn,* made 4/13/88, 3"h x 3"l. $35-40. *Courtesy of Ben Curtis.*

Farm animals by Boyd and Mosser. The Mosser pig has an "M". The standing Mosser pig, c.1990s, is 2.5"h x 2.75"l. $20-24. Boyd's *Suee Pig,* made 4/5/88, is 2"h x 3"l. $30-32. Boyd's *Mabel Cow,* made late 1990s, is 2.25"h x 4"l. $18-20. *Courtesy of Ben Curtis.*

Boyd animals. First row left to right *Andy Bear,* made in the late 1990s, is 3"h. $15-18. *Willie Mouse,* made 5/22/91, is 2"h. $22-25. *Patrick Balloon Bear,* made 5/29/91, is 2.2"h. $22-25. *Jeremy Frog,* made 10/2/92, is 1.25"h x 2.2"l. $22-25. *Artie Penguin,* made 9/14/92, is 2.75"h. $22-25. *Bernie Eagle,* made 9/17/92, is 2.5"h. $22-25. *Pete Pelican,* made 7/9/96, is 2.75"h. $18-20. Back row left to right *Dog* pencil holder, made in the late 1990s, is 1.7"h. $14-16. *Skippy Dog,* made 7/31/96, is 3"h. $22-25. *Bull Dog's Head,* made 5/16/95, is 3.2"h. $22-25. *"JB" Scotty Dog,* made 4/20/88, is 3.2"h. $28-30. *Miss Cotton the Kitten,* made 5/3/94, is 2.5"h. $18-20. *Courtesy of Ben Curtis.*

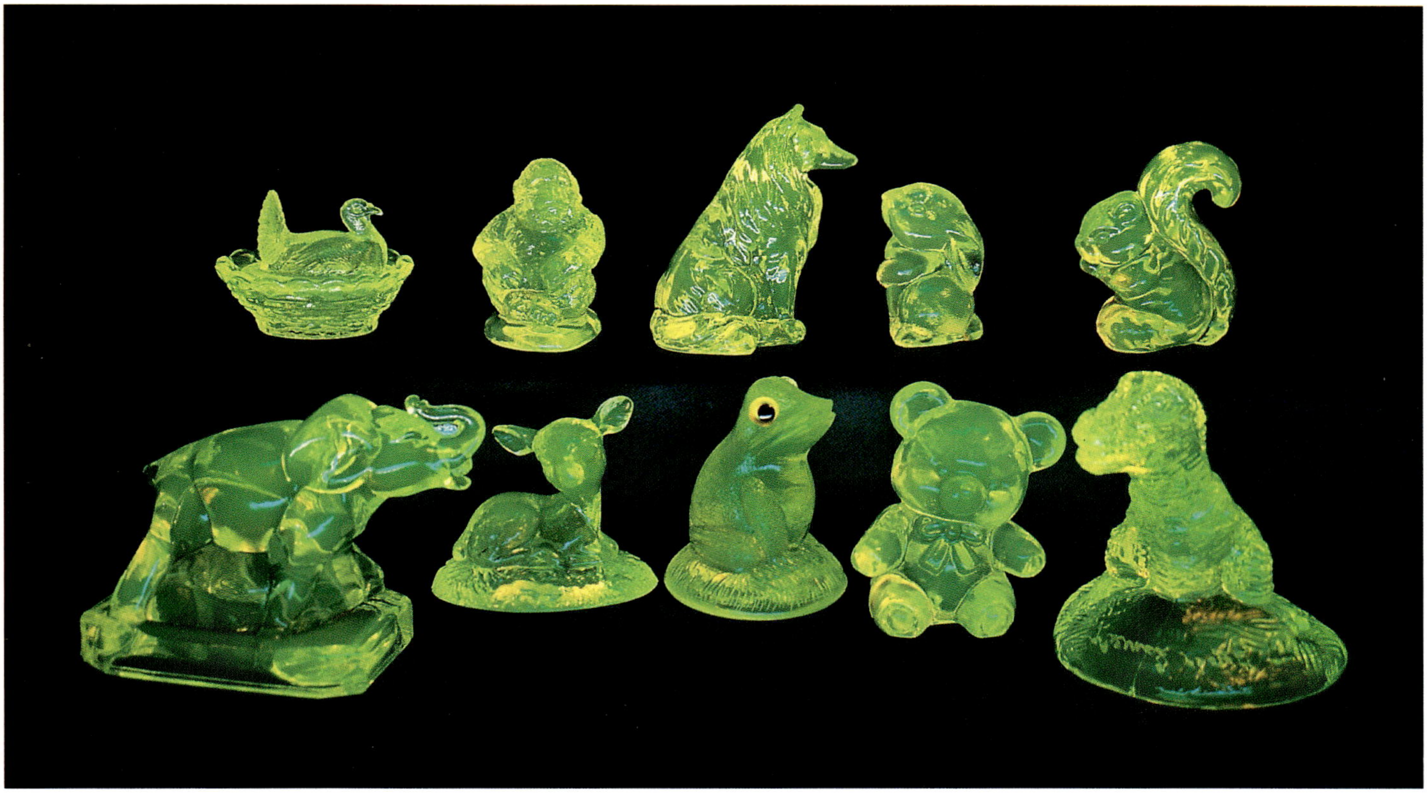

Boyd and Summit Art Glass: Front row left to right *Zack Elephant*, made 5/23/94, is 3.3"h x 3.5"l. $28-30. *Bingo Deer*, made 5/12/94, is 2.2"h x 2.6"l. $22-25. Frog by Summit Art Glass, in early 1990s, is 2.75"h. $18-20. *Fuzzy Bear*, made 4/6/88, is 2.75"h. $32-35. *Rex Dinosaur*, made 5/5/94, is 4"h x 3.5"b. This particular dinosaur is signed by Bernard Boyd. $40-45. Back row left to right *Turkey salt*, made 4/25/94, is 1.9"h x 2.5"l. $20-23. *Sonny Gorilla*, made 5/25/94, is 2.3"h. $22-25. *Lassie* made by Mosser in the 1990s, is 3"h. $28-30. *Brian Bunny*, made 4/11/88, is 2"h. $32-35. *Sammy Squirrel*, made 6/12/91, is 2.7"h. $32-35. *Courtesy of Ben Curtis.*

Boyd dolls. The small dolls in the front are left to right: *Elizabeth*, made 5/14/91, is 2.4"h. $28-30. *Nancy*, made 7/12/96, is 2.1"h $24-26. The large dolls in the back are left to right: *Marguerite*, made 6/12/91, is 4.3"h. $32-35. *Colonial Man*, made 4/18/88, is 4.2"h. $32-35. *Louise*, made 9/8/80, is 4.5"h. The color of this piece was originally called Firefly. $40-42. *Courtesy of Molly Curtis.*

An *Owl* candy dish by Summitt Art Glass, c.1990s. 6.5"h x 3.5"b. $30-35. A Santa Sleigh candy dish, 4.5"h x 5.3"l. Maker unknown, c.1990s. This is a Westmoreland mold. $40-45. *Courtesy of Ben Curtis.*

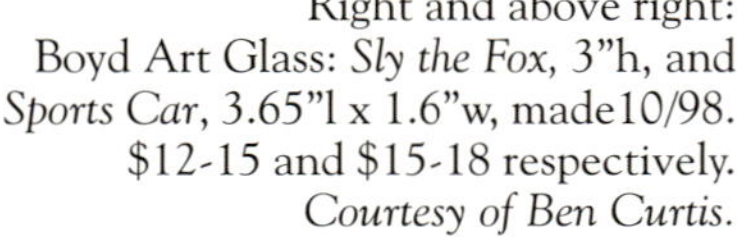

Right and above right: Boyd Art Glass: *Sly the Fox,* 3"h, and *Sports Car,* 3.65"l x 1.6"w, made10/98. $12-15 and $15-18 respectively. *Courtesy of Ben Curtis.*

Boyd Art Glass: Left to right: *Cupid,* made 1990s, 3"h. $15-18. *Pressed Bird,* made 4/8/88, is 2.75"h. $18-20. *Tommy Tiger,* made 5/23/95, is 1.5"h x 2.5"l. $22-25. *Turtle,* made 4/5/88, 1"h x 2.8"l. $22-25. *Courtesy of Ben Curtis.*

Boyd Art Glass: Left to right: The *Boyd Mirror*, made 4/26/88, is 8.25"l x 4.5"w. $40-45. *Katie Butterfly*, made 5/28/91, is 2"l x 2.8"w. $15-18. *Child's Covered Dish*, made 4/20/88, is 3.25"h x 2.7"d. $27-30.

Toothpicks, makers unknown, c.1980s-1990s. Front row left to right: Square candleholder or toothpick, 2"h x 2.2"sq. $22-25. A satin glass toothpick in shape of flower pot, 2.6"h x 2.7"w. $25-28. *Daisy and Button* satin glass toothpick, 2.7"h x 2"w. $25-28. *Daisy and Button* opalescent toothpick, 2.65"h x 2"w. $25-28. An eye cup, 2.65"h. $28-35.

Boyd Art Glass: The *Hoppy Toothpick*, made 6/1/95, is one of Boyd's specialty items. It is a limited edition, 671/1000. $35-40. The *Hat Toothpick*, made 4/8/88, is 2.25"h. $22-25. The *Daisy and Button Toothpick*, made 6/25/91, is 2.5"h. $20-22. The *Basket Toothpick*, made 4/29/80, is 2"h. $30-32. The *Mini Vase Toothpick*, made 9/5/80, is 2.5"h. $30-32.

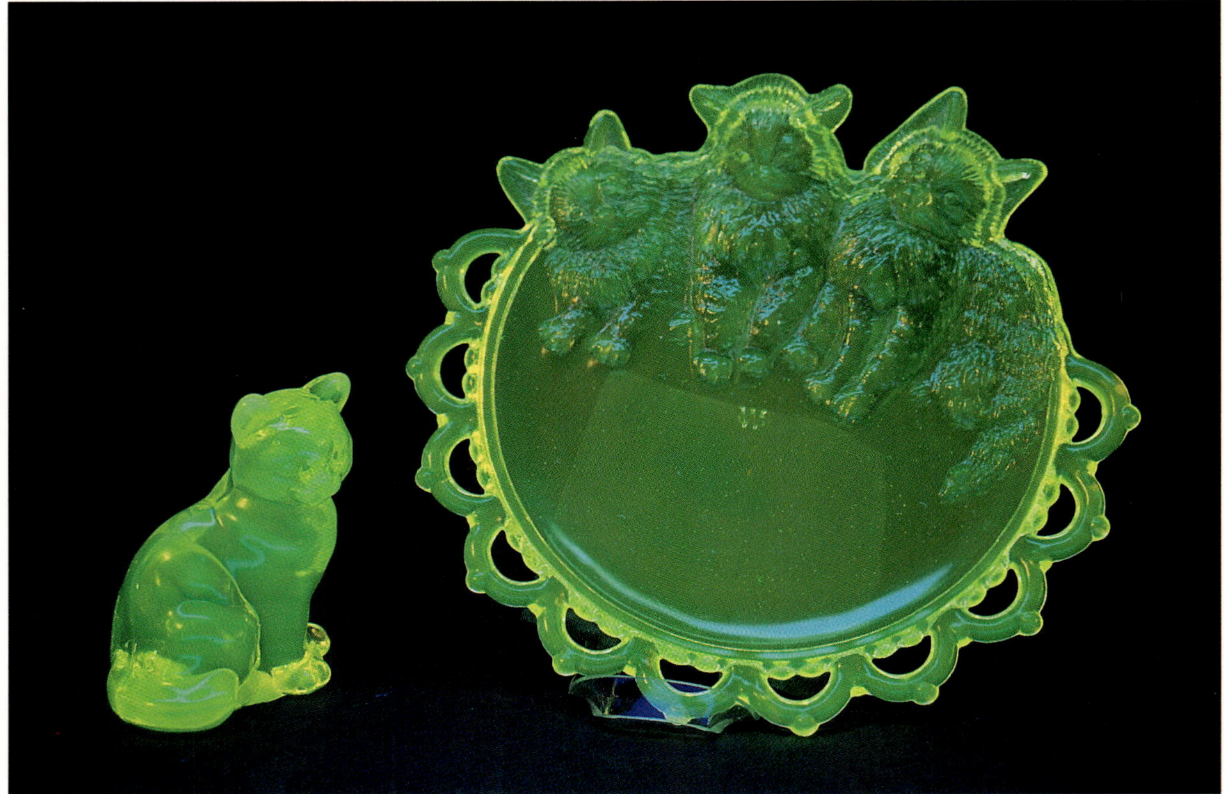

A Fenton opalescent cat, c.1980s, 3.5"h. $40-45. An 8" cat plate made from a Westmoreland mold. It has the "W" with a "G" on top. Maker unknown, c.1990s. $45-50.

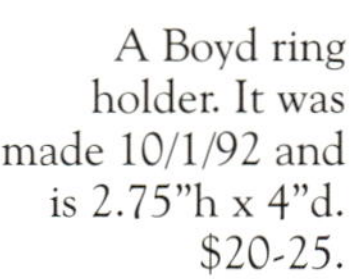

Front row left to right: A flared top toothpick, maker and date unknown, 2.4"h x 1.1"w. $22-25. This large toothpick, 2.4"h x 2.75"w, with it's branch-like trim could be used as a candleholder. Maker and c. unknown. $20-25. A S *Repeat* reproduction toothpick, 1.35"h x 1.85"w. Maker and c. unknown. $20-24. Back row left to right: An *Indian Head* toothpick by Rosso, c.1990s, 2.75"h x 1.95"w. $20-22. A *Doghouse* toothpick, maker unknown, c.1990s, 2.5"h x 2.25"w. $20-24. Boyd *Texas Boot* toothpick, made 6/28/91, 2.7"h x 1.75"w. $22-25.

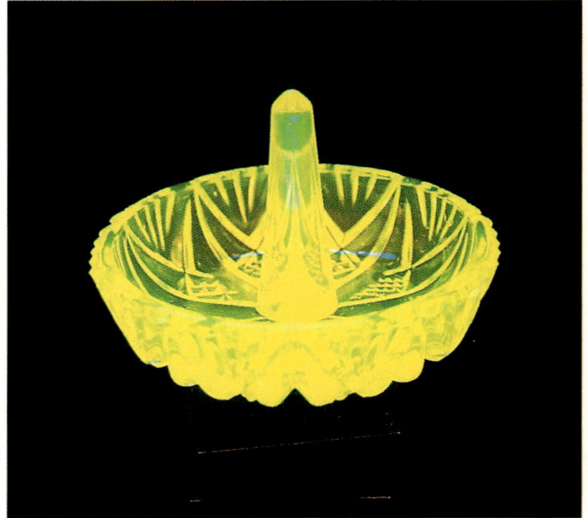

A Boyd ring holder. It was made 10/1/92 and is 2.75"h x 4"d. $20-25.

Colonial Bow slippers. The iridescent slipper on the left is made by Boyd, c.1988. $28-30. The other is Degenhart, c.1972. $55-65. They measure 2.25"h x 5.5"l. *Courtesy of Laura Kelm and Pete Buck.*

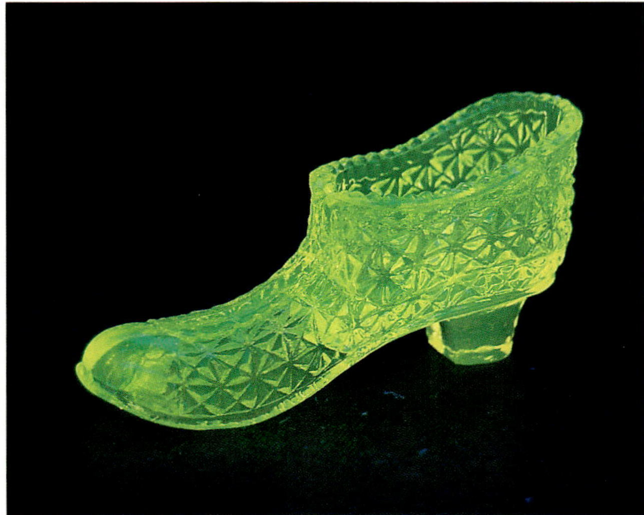

Degenhart's Miniature Slipper, c.1966.
This slipper has a beaded edge at the
top and a hollowed sole. Before 1966
the mold had a full sole with tread
marks. $45-50. *Courtesy of Laura Kelm
and Pete Buck.*

Boyd plate, July 1, 1991. This
portrait plate of Bernard C. Boyd
is 5"d. $50-60. *Courtesy of Laura
Kelm and Pete Buck.*

A group of Degenhart Toothpicks. The
pieces made before 1972 do not have
the "D" inside the Heart logo. Front
row left to right, *Bird toothpick*, c.1959,
2.75"h. *Forget-Me-Not toothpick*,
c.1965, 2.5"h. *Heart toothpick*, c.1972,
2.6"h. Back row left to right, *Mini
pitcher toothpick*, c.1974, 2.2"h. *Gypsy
Kettle toothpick*, c.1972, 2.25"h. *Beaded
Oval toothpick*, c.1967, 2.65"h. $65-75
ea. Each of these molds has been made
in vaseline by Boyd Art Glass since
1980. The Boyd pieces will be marked
with the Boyd logo.

A group of Degenhart salts. *Daisy and
Button salt*, c.1972, 1.5"h. *Pottie salt*,
c.1972, 1.5"h. *Bird salt*, c.1958, 1.6"h.
$55-60 ea. Each of these molds has
been made by Boyd Art Glass.

A group of Degenhart novelties. *Degenhart Owl*, c.1968, 3.6"h, $115-125. The Degenhart logo is a script "D" on the bottom of this mold. *Bicentennial Bell*, c.1976, 2"h. $35-45. *Hobo Shoe*, c.1972, 2"h. $55-75.

Two Degenhart novelties. A Heart Jewel Box, c.1972, 1.2"h x 3.5"l x 3.75"w. $60-75. The 3" Hen, c.1973. $55-75.

A Degenhart and a Summit doll. Degenhart's *Priscilla* on the left was made between June 1976 and April 1978. She is 5"h and is marked on the back base with the Degenhart logo, a capital "D" inside a heart. $125-150. The doll on the right is *Melanie* by Summit Art Glass. She is 5"h and made of slag glass. She is marked on the back with the Summit logo, a capital "V" inside a circle, and "S. B." This mold was reportedly broken in the early 1980s. $100-125.

A group of Boyd dolls. *Louise*, the doll on the left, is the annual bell that Boyd makes in this particular mold. This vaseline carnival bell was made 8/27/96 and is 4.25"h. $35-37. The middle dolls are an Amish couple. *Sara* is 2.2"h and *Eli* is 2.3"h. They were made 7/8/96. $28-30 pair. The doll on the right is *Jennifer*, made 7/19/96, 3.7"h. $22-25.

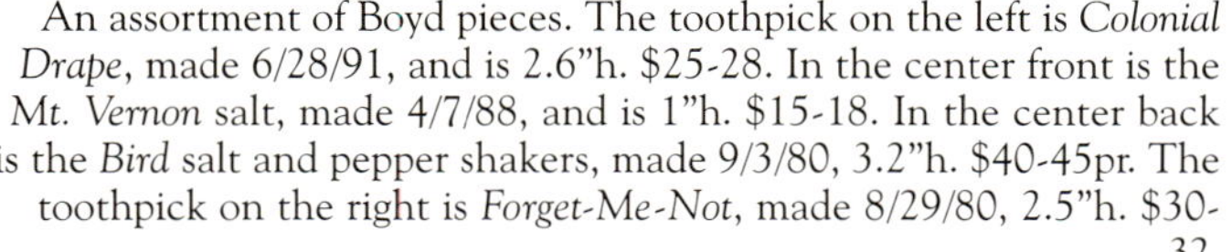

An assortment of Boyd pieces. The toothpick on the left is *Colonial Drape*, made 6/28/91, and is 2.6"h. $25-28. In the center front is the *Mt. Vernon* salt, made 4/7/88, and is 1"h. $15-18. In the center back is the *Bird* salt and pepper shakers, made 9/3/80, 3.2"h. $40-45pr. The toothpick on the right is *Forget-Me-Not*, made 8/29/80, 2.5"h. $30-32.

Boyd angels. These angels are 4.5"h and were made 6/25/95. The left angel is a front view of the mold. The right angel is a back view and is vaseline carnival . $20-22 ea.

A group of swans. The swan on the left is made by Mosser and marked with a "M" inside a shield, 3.75"l. $18-20. Notice the difference in the curve of the neck as compared to the Boyd swans. The center swan is the Boyd 4.5" vaseline carnival swan, made 8/21/96. $22-25. The right swan is the Boyd 3" vaseline carnival swan, made 8/21/96. $18-20.

Left:
Boyd candy dishes. On the left is Boyd's *Butterpat* candy dish, made 4/27/88, and is 6"h x 4.65"d. $43-45. On the right is Boyd's *Honey Jar* candy dish, made 6/8/95 and is 4.75"h x 3.75"b. Notice the bees. $35-38.

Boyd puff boxes. The novelty on the left is the *Rose Puff Box*, made 5/24/95, 2.9"h x 4.1"d. $30-32. The novelty on the right is the *Boyd Puff Box*, made 6/13/91, 2.3"h x 4"d. $33-35.

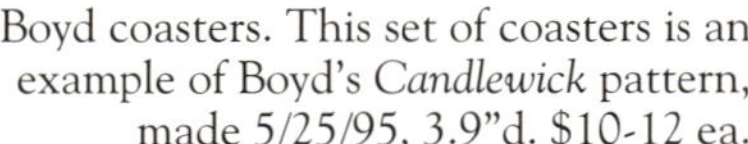

Boyd coasters. This set of coasters is an example of Boyd's *Candlewick* pattern, made 5/25/95, 3.9"d. $10-12 ea.

Boyd's *Dog Head* on the left was made 6/1/95, 3.6"h. $18-20. In the center is a mushroom paperweight possibly made by Degenhart, 3.6"h. $40-45. On the right is Boyd's *Bowling Pin Ashtray*, made 8/5/96, 3"l. $14-16.

Boyd Art Glass: The paperweight with a flower inside, made 6/3/95, is a special edition. It is marked with a script "B" on the bottom, 2.6"h x 3"d. $75-80. The *Grape Cardholder*, made 4/21/88, is 2.6"h x 3"l x 1.4"w. $30-32. The *Boyd Logo*, made 9/3/80, is 3"l x 2.5"w. $38-40.

Boyd Art Glass: *Aunt Sheila's Pin Dish*, made 5/13/94, is 5"l x 4"w. $22-25. The 5" *Hen*, made 9/12/80, $32-35.

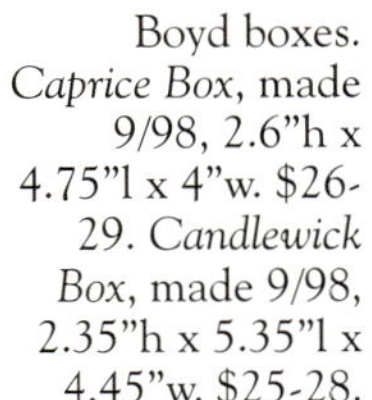

Boyd boxes. *Caprice Box*, made 9/98, 2.6"h x 4.75"l x 4"w. $26-29. *Candlewick Box*, made 9/98, 2.35"h x 5.35"l x 4.45"w. $25-28.

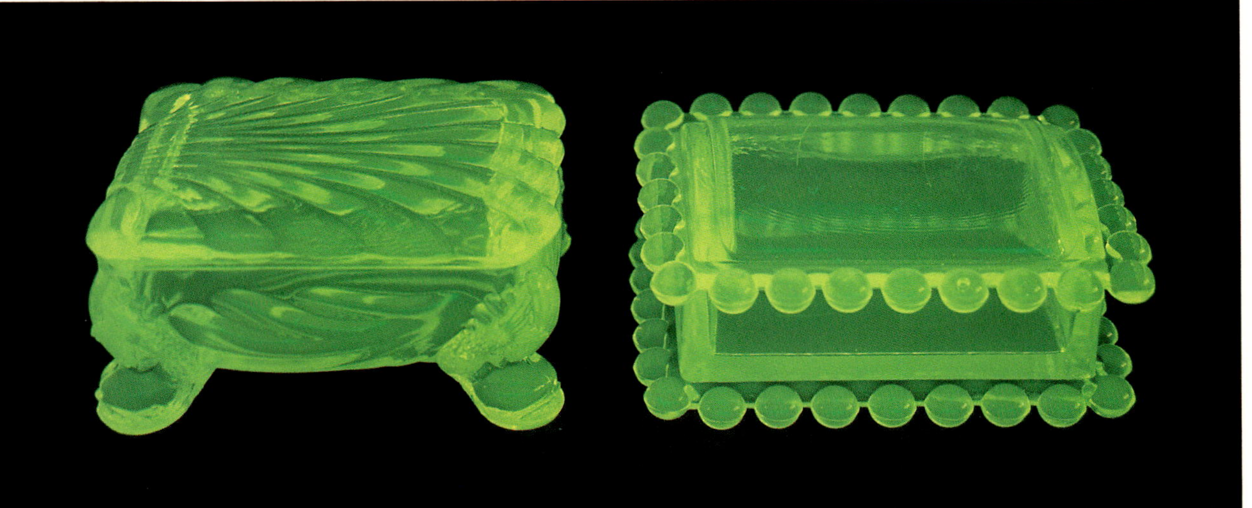

Left:
Boyd *Christmas Bell*, made 1997, 6"h x 3.8"d. $25-30.

Right:
Vaseline marbles, maker unknown, and Boyd marble holders, c.1990s. One of the large 2" marbles has opalescent stripes, the other has streaks resembling etching. $125-150 ea. The 1" marble in the center is solid vaseline. $60-75. The .5" marbles are frosted vaseline. $35-50 ea. The marble holders leaning against the stands are 1.6"d. $12-15 ea. *Courtesy of Connie Curtis.*

Dolls by Vi Hunter, c.1980s. The dolls are slag vaseline. Jenny is 4.2"h. Josh is 4.4"h. $40-45 ea. Miniature Jenny is 2.15"h. $25-35.

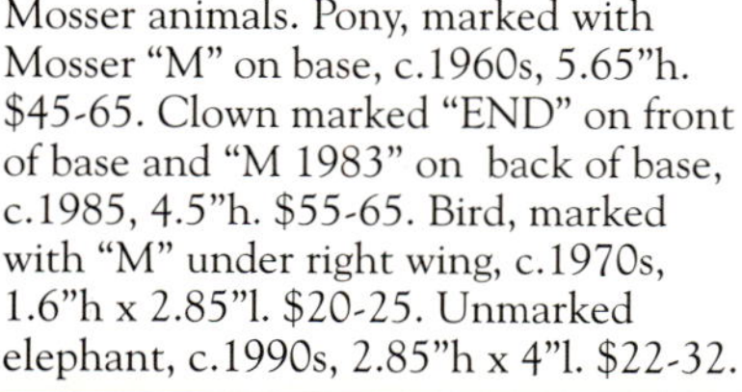

Mosser animals. Pony, marked with Mosser "M" on base, c.1960s, 5.65"h. $45-65. Clown marked "END" on front of base and "M 1983" on back of base, c.1985, 4.5"h. $55-65. Bird, marked with "M" under right wing, c.1970s, 1.6"h x 2.85"l. $20-25. Unmarked elephant, c.1990s, 2.85"h x 4"l. $22-32.

A bride's basket by Gibson, c.1990s. This iridescent bowl with heavy opalescent around the top is in a silver-plate holder, bowl is 3.6"h x 8"d. $350-375.

A decanter possibly by Gibson, c.1990s. This ribbed, blown, opalescent decanter has an iridescent finish, 8.5"h x 4.5"d x 2.5"b. $200-225.

A heart design cruet possibly by Gibson, c.1990s. This blown cruet with the hanging heart design is 7.25"h x 2.75"d. $195-220.

A group of cruets by Gibson, c.1990s. These are blown cruets with varying degrees of opalescence and iridescence. The cruet on the left is 7"h x 3.25"d. The center cruet is 6.5"h x 3.5"d. and the thumbprint pattern cruet on the right is 7.5"h x 3"d. $150-175 ea.

A spittoon possibly by Gibson, c. 1990s. This blown, opalescent, crackle glass spittoon or vase is 3.75"h x 3.65"d. $95-125.

An apple paperweight possibly by Gibson, c.1990s. This pretty opalescent apple paperweight is 4.25"h x 2.7"d. $75-90.

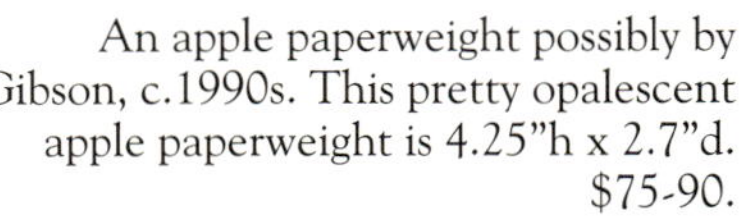

A compote, maker unknown, c.1990s. This iridescent, flower shaped compote is 4.3"h x 3.65"b. $50-75.

A rooster candy dish made by Boyd for Rosso, c.1990s. This footed, rooster candy dish is 5.5"h x 2.5"b. $45-60.

A flower shaped novelty possibly by Gibson, c.1990s. This flower with opalescent petals is 5.3"l x 3.75"d. $35-55.

A candy cane novelty, maker unknown, c.1990s. It is 5.6"l. $15-20.

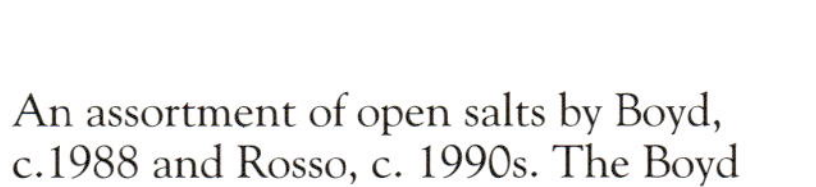

An assortment of open salts by Boyd, c.1988 and Rosso, c. 1990s. The Boyd salt is second from the left, $15-18. The other three salts $12-18 ea.

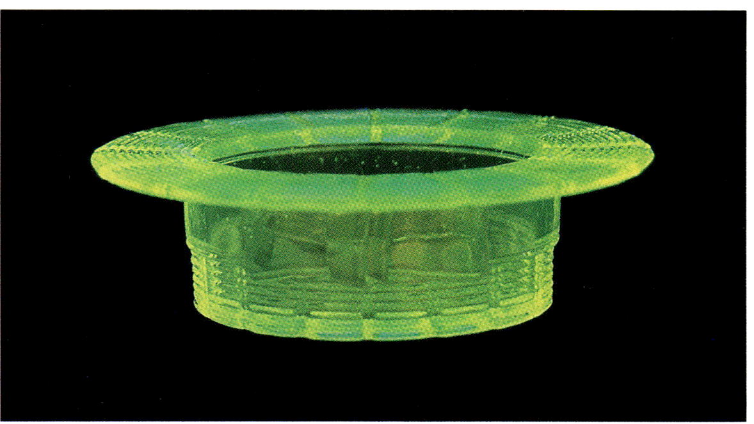

Top hat by Summit Art Glass, c.1995. This straw top hat is 1.25"h x 4.25"l. $25-30. *Courtesy of Laura Kelm and Pete Buck.*

Ring holders, maker unknown, c.1990s. These opalescent pieces can be used as ring holders or paperweights. They measure left 3.4"h x 2.05"w and right 3.85"h x 1.95"w. $50-65.

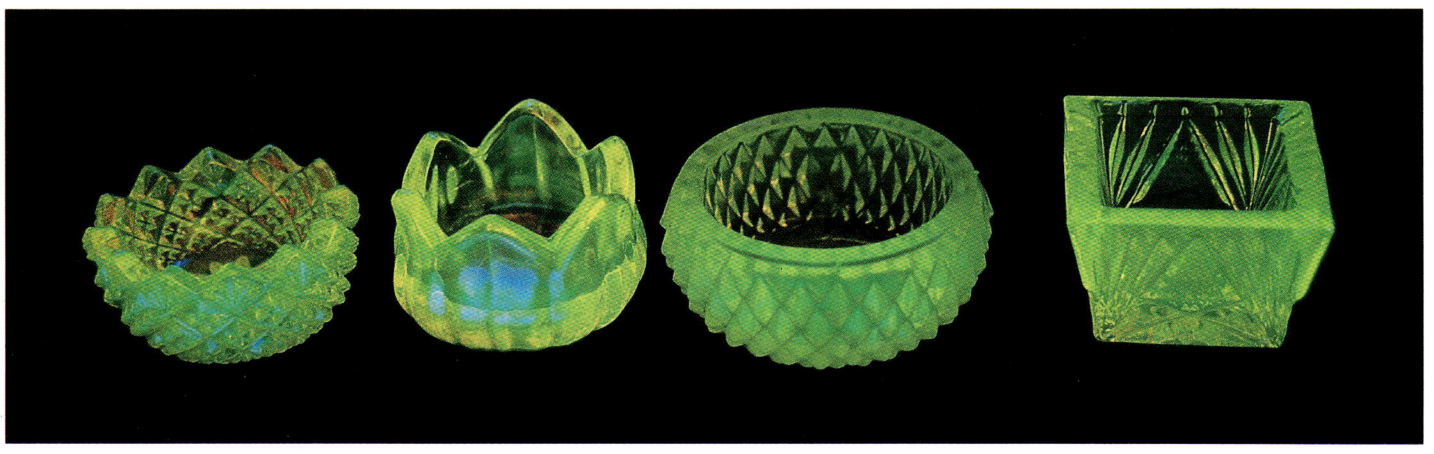

A watch novelty, maker unknown, c.1990s. This pocket watch has a deer head on the front, 2.13"d. $65-75.

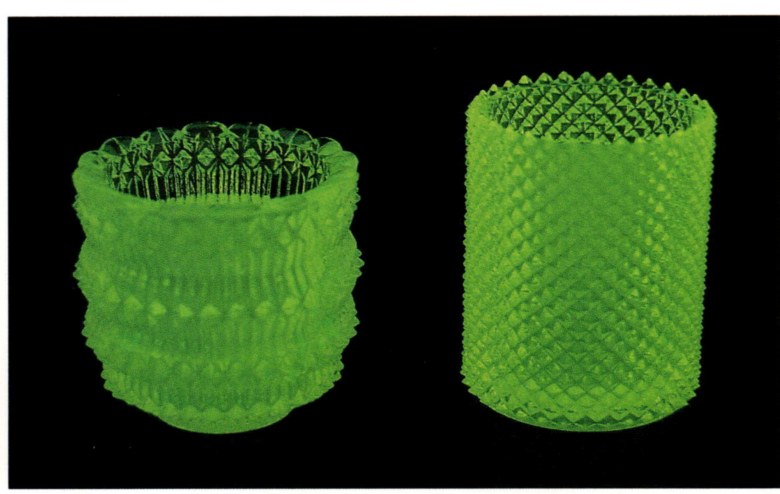

Faroy candleholders. The taller diamond pattern candleholder is marked with patent No. 204, 556, 2.75"h. The shorter one is marked with patent No. 235,469, 2.25"h. $25-30 ea. *Courtesy of Laura Kelm and Pete Buck.*

A perfume bottle possibly by Gibson, c.1990s. This pretty opalescent fan shaped perfume bottle is iridescent and is 5.1"h x 3.75"w. $95-125.

A clown disk. This is a very small, 1.75"d, opalescent disc with a clown in the center that resembles Mosser's "Jiggs". The inscription around the disc reads "All The World Loves A Clown". $50-75. *Courtesy of Laura Kelm and Pete Buck.*

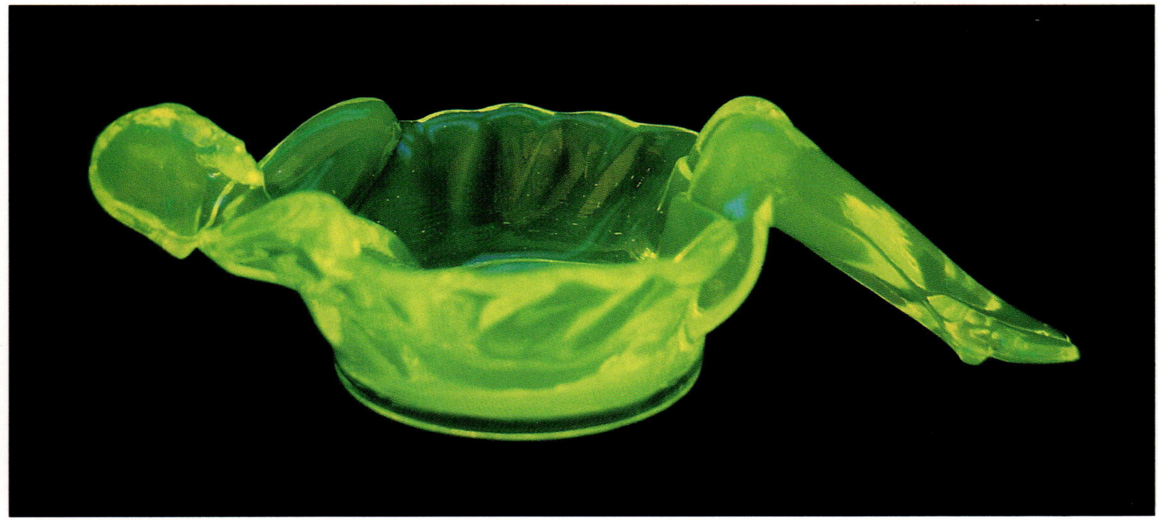

Ballerina dish, made from a Westmoreland mold in 1980s. 8.75"l x 4.5"w. $50-75. *Courtesy of Laura Kelm and Pete Buck.*

A miniature plate, 3.4"d, with a rose in the center and "Yellow Rose" around the top and "Texas" around the bottom. $40-50. *Courtesy of Laura Kelm and Pete Buck.*

Heisey miniature plate, c. unknown. This small, 3.4"d, plate has a pitcher in the center and is inscribed with "National Heisey Glass Museum Newark, Ohio" around the edge. $40-50. *Courtesy of Laura Kelm and Pete Buck.*

Above and left: *Ring and Petal* table set by Rosso, c.1998. The covered sugar is 6.5"h, the covered butter is 5.75"h, the spooner is 4"h, and the creamer is 4.25"h. $20-22ea. *Courtesy of Laura Kelm and Pete Buck.*

Fenton cat, c.1998. This hand painted cat is 3.5"h. $35-45. *Courtesy of Laura Kelm and Pete Buck.*

Two child's cups. The one in the front is *Heron and Pheasant* by Degenhart, c.1960s. 2.6"h x 2.5"d. $50-75. The one in the back has a dog and cat design and the Mosser marking on the bottom, c. 1980s. 2.75"h x 2.5"d. $35-55.

Right: A measuring cup, maker unknown, c.1980s. This vaseline measuring cup is made from a depression era mold, 4.45"h x 3"d. $30-45.

An opalescent Fenton bear, 3.5"h, c.1990s. $40-45. *Courtesy of Larry and Lois Smith.*

Right: An *Open Rose* bowl and butter dish. Maker unknown, c.1990s. These pieces are carnival vaseline and made from Imperial Glass molds. They have the Imperial Glass "IG" plus a big "V" at the bottom of the logo. The 3 footed bowl is 3.65"h x 6.25"d. $48-62. The covered butter dish is 5.75"h x 7.5"d. $75-85.

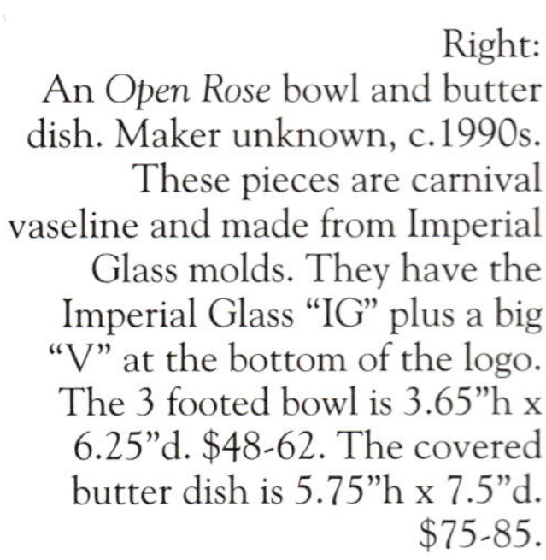

An *Open Rose* creamer and sugar. The creamer is 7.5"h x 3.5"w and the open sugar is 4.6"h x 4.25"w. $48-62ea. See previous photo.

Embossed Rose fairy light by L. G. Wright, c.1960s. 6"h x 5.65"b. $90-110.

A pair of candleholders made from a Westmoreland mold for Rosso, c.1990s. 3.85"h x 4.1"b. $75-95 pair.

Daisy and Button candleholders. This pair of footed, opalescent, *Daisy and Button* candleholders was made by Fenton for L. G. Wright, c.1960s. They measure 2.6"h x 5.4"l. $50-75 ea.

A *Bird Cage* candy dish, maker unknown, c. late 1980s-early 1990s. This is an Imperial Glass mold. It has the Imperial logo I with G on top plus a backward L to the right. Notice the birds on the perches. 5.5"h x 4.75"d. $120-160.

Boyd *High Boot*, made 10/98, 4.15"h x 4.6"l. $16-20.

Chapter V.
Vaseline Glass from Europe

English compote, maker unknown, c.1898. Heacock named the pattern of this compote *Queen's Crown*, 6.0"h x 8.5"d. The registry number is 320124. $275-300.

A *William and Mary* oval bowl, 6.5"h x 4.75"d. $100-125.

An English celery vase, maker unknown possibly Davidson, c.1901. This pattern is *William and Mary*, registry number 413701, 5.75"h x 4.5"d. $225-250.

A *William and Mary* oval bowl, 8.5"h x 6.25"d. $150-175.

A *William and Mary* creamer and waste bowl. Creamer 4.7"h x 2.9"d. $150-175. Waste bowl 2.75"h x 5"d. $175-195.

An English divided sweet by Davidson and Co., c.1889. The pattern of this canary opalescent piece is *Richelieu*, 8.5"l x 7.25"w. There is no registry number. $150-175.

An oval English plate, maker unknown, c.1896. The unidentified pattern of this very dark yellow plate can be dated by the registry number, 254027, 8.5"l x 6.5"w. $100-125.

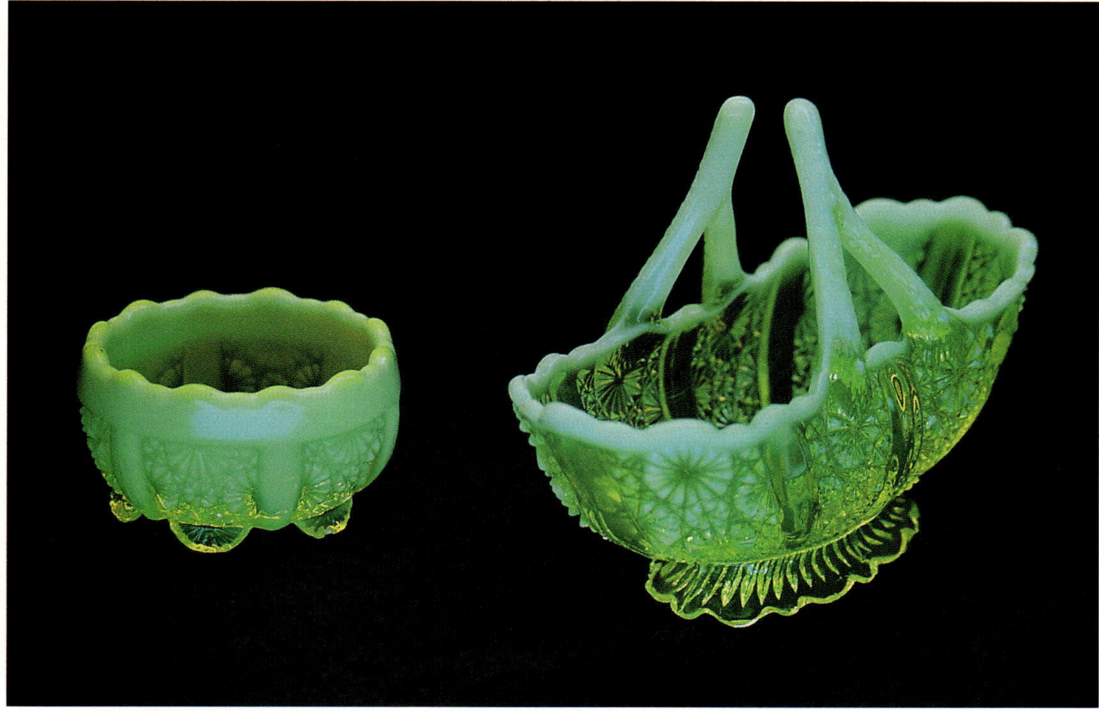

An English basket and master salt by George Davidson and Co., c.1891. This pattern is *Lady Chippendale* and has the registry number 176566. Basket, 6"l x 2.35"w. $125-150. Master salt, 1.5"h x 2.6"d. $95-115.

A *Lady Chippendale* butter dish, 4.5"h x
7"d. *Courtesy of Larry and Lois Smith.*
$300-350.

Lady Chippendale nut dishes, 1.5"h x
5"d. $85-95 ea.

An English open sugar and creamer,
maker unknown, c.1890. This pattern
is called *Quilted Pillow Sham* by
Heacock. There is no registry number.
Open sugar, 3.25"h x 7"l x 5"w.
Creamer, 4"h x 3.5"w. $150-175 ea.

Single lily epergne, maker unknown, possibly English, c.1890s. The opalescent lily has a fishnet or waffle-like pattern. The epergne is 10"h x 4.4"b. $200-250.

A *Princess Diana* platter by George Davidson and Co., c.1885-1890. This typical English platter is 10.25"l x 8"w. $225-250. *Courtesy of Larry and Lois Smith.*

War of Roses bowl by George Davidson and Company, c.1879. The heavy opalescence of this boat-shaped bowl is typical of English opalescent glass. The registry number in the bottom of this piece is 212684. The bowl and stand measure 5.75"h x 6"l. $200-225. *Courtesy of Laura Kelm and Pete Buck.*

Sweetmeat server, maker unknown, c.1800s. This beautiful sweetmeat server is most likely English. The glass has a light opalescence around the edge and is very delicate. Notice the unusual design of the silver-plate stand. The base is engraved with a "CL". 6"h x 8.75"d. $300-350.

Left and below:
A compote by Vallerysthal, c.1930s. This French made compote has very detailed design on the leaf plate and the tree trunk pedestal and base. Vallerysthal is molded on the side of the plate. Two views are shown for detail. 4.75"h x 8.75"d. $275-300.

A cigarette stand by Vallerysthal, c.1930s. This cigarette stand is marked "France P. V." on the bottom. It is sometimes referred to as Rip Van Winkle "sleeping boy". 3"h x 4.75"l. $100-125.

A pair of vases, maker and circa unknown. The owner of these vases reported that they were purchased in England during the early 1940s. They measure 6"h x 2.75"d. $125-150 ea. *Courtesy of Laura Kelm and Pete Buck.*

Victorian vase, maker unknown, c.1890s. This Victorian vase is a very pale Vaseline with opalescent stripes. The flower is part cranberry and part white. The leaves are a darker Vaseline. 7.5"h. $150-175.
Courtesy of Larry and Lois Smith.

A beautiful pair of double-handled Victorian vases in vaseline. They have opalescent tops with blue rims and the applied flowers are cranberry. They measure 11.25"h x 4.1"b. $1400-1500 pr. *Courtesy of Larry and Lois Smith.*

Tulip vase. This blown Victorian tulip vase has a cranberry top, maker unknown, c.1890s. 7"h x 2.5"b. $225-250.

A *Rubina Verde* condiment dish, maker unknown, c.1880s. This swirled pattern *Rubina Verde* condiment dish has a canary applied edge and rigaree. The silver-plated stand is marked Beresford Plate K5199 EPNS B/4050. The bowl is 2.4"h x 5.4"d. The stand is 5.75"h x 6.5"d. $350-375.

Jack-in-Pulpit vase. The maker of this blown *Jack-in-Pulpit* vase is unknown, c.1890s, $75-85.

This beautiful Art Glass bowl with it's ruffled, peach colored top is possibly Stevens and Williams, c.1890s. Notice the design inside the bowl, 6"d. $300-350. *Courtesy of Laura Kelm and Pete Buck.*

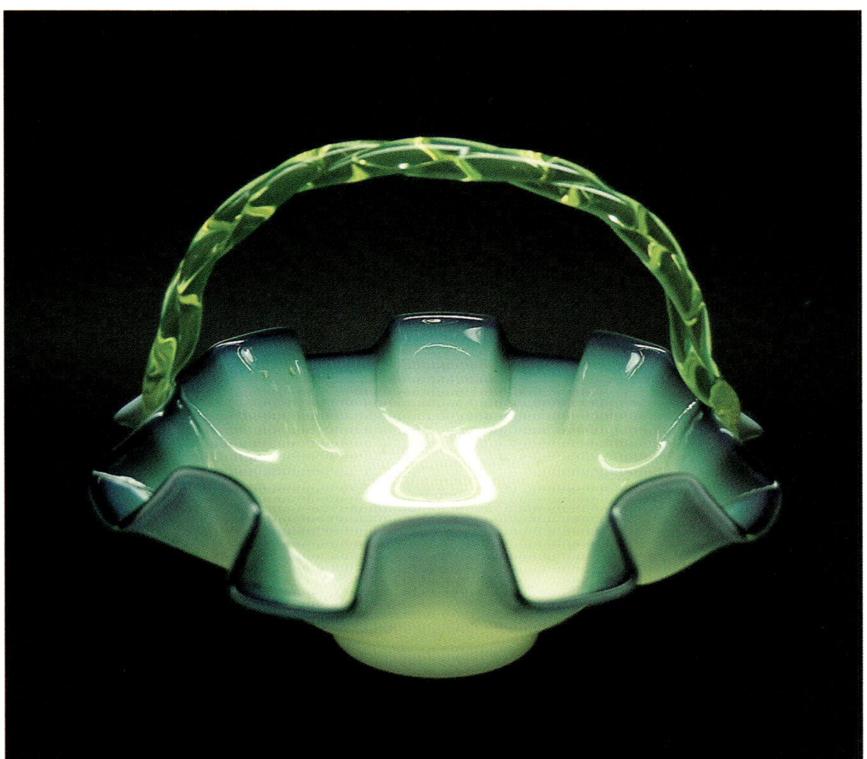

An English Art Glass basket, maker possibly Stevens and Williams, c.1890s. This attractive 8" basket is made of 3 cased colors of glass, canary, white, and blue. $450-500. *Courtesy of Laura Kelm and Pete Buck.*

An Art Glass rose bowl, maker possibly Stevens and Williams, c.1890s. This unusual 6" rose bowl is a very light amber at the bottom, and amethyst at the top. The applied leaves are canary. $325-375. *Courtesy of Laura Kelm and Pete Buck.*

Art Glass, maker unknown, possibly English, c.1890s. This beautiful piece of art glass is a purple lily with opalescent petals and 2 canary leaves for the legs, 6"h. $275-300. *Courtesy of Laura Kelm and Pete Buck.*

An amethyst basket, maker possibly Stevens and Williams, c.1890s. This 5" amethyst art glass basket has a vaseline top in the shape of leaves and a vaseline handle. $375-400. *Courtesy of Laura Kelm and Pete Buck.*

An art glass basket, maker possibly
Stevens and Williams, c.1890s. This cased
basket is vaseline with white. The top is
crimped, and the applied handle and
leaves are vaseline. The applied flowers
are cranberry. 4"h x 4"w x 7"l. $375-400.
Courtesy of Laura Kelm and Pete Buck.

Rubina Verde bowl. The maker of this
piece of English art glass is unknown,
c. 1890s. The photo is taken to show
the threaded pattern and the applied
rigaree, 2"h x 5.25"d. $150-175.
Courtesy of Laura Kelm and Pete Buck.

A blown vase, maker and circa
unknown, possibly 1900s. This 3"
opalescent blown geometric design rose
bowl has a light cranberry top. $175-
200. *Courtesy of Laura Kelm and Pete
Buck.*

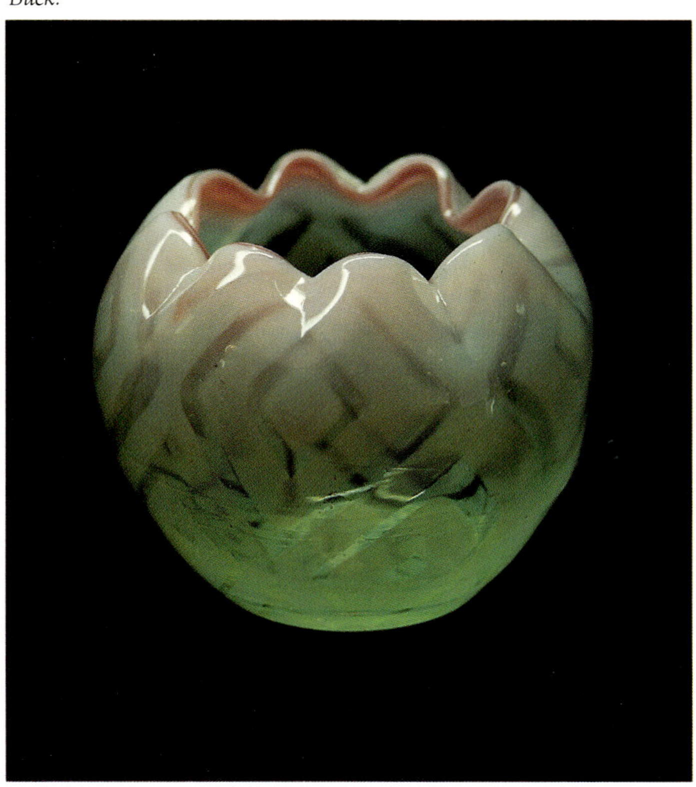

An opalescent cup, maker unknown,
c.1890s. This opalescent swirled cup
with pink applied handle and feet is
possibly English art glass. $80-100.
Courtesy of Laura Kelm and Pete Buck.

Murano Bird, c.1950s. This bird can be used as a paperweight, 2"h x 3.25"l. $65-75. *Courtesy of Laura Kelm and Pete Buck.*

Italian perfume, c.1930s. The label on this atomizer identifies it as Stiver, Italy. 4"h x 3.25"b. $200-250.

Czech vase. This is an example of Czechoslovakian art glass. The maker and circa are unknown. $200-250. *Courtesy of Melanie Schonier.*

Decanter, maker and circa unknown.
This unusual tall long-necked vaseline
decanter decorated with a variety of
colored enameled flecks is possibly
Czechoslovakian. $500-550. *Courtesy of
Melanie Schonier.*

Murano Poodle. This poodle by Murano,
c.1950s, is made of two colors of glass,
red glass cased in vaseline. Eyes, nose,
and tongue are also red. $175-200.
Courtesy of Melanie Schonier.

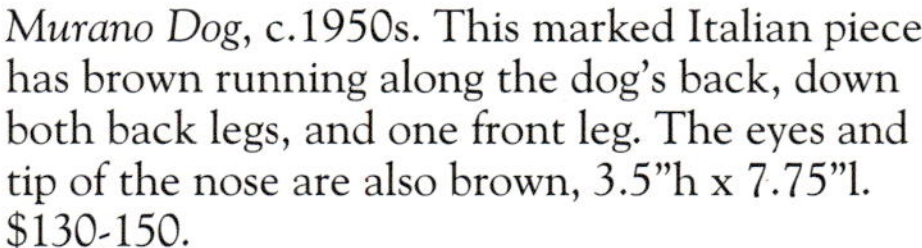

Murano Geese, c.1950s. These two Murano geese are made of cased red and vaseline glass. The large one is 8.5"h, and the small one is 6.25"h. $185-200 ea. *Courtesy of Laura Kelm and Pete Buck.*

Murano Dog, c.1950s. This marked Italian piece has brown running along the dog's back, down both back legs, and one front leg. The eyes and tip of the nose are also brown, 3.5"h x 7.75"l. $130-150.

Murano Birds. This unusual piece by Murano, c.1950s has two birds perched on a clear branch. The birds are made of blue and vaseline glass. The vaseline is most evident in the bird's tails. $225-250. *Courtesy of Melanie Schonier.*

Murano Poodle, c.1950s. This cute poodle has a blue body and feet with a red nose and eyes to compliment the vaseline. 8.5"h x 4.5"l, $175-200. *Courtesy of Laura Kelm and Pete Buck.*

Murano Swan, c.1950s. This little swan with it's orange beak and comb is typical of this Italian glass manufacturer. 5"h x 3.5"l x 1.5"w. $120-140. *Courtesy of Laura Kelm and Pete Buck.*

A bowl and under plate, maker and circa unknown, possibly Czechoslovakian. The plate and bowl are trimmed in gold. Orange, red, blue, and gold are the colors used to hand paint the unusual alternating design on these pieces. The bottoms of these pieces have a sunburst design and are ground smooth. The vaseline color is very dark. The bowl is 2.6"h x 5.5"d, and the plate is 6.5"d. $175-225 set.

An English blown vase, c.1890s. This blown vase is 4.25"h and very delicate. The fluted top is trimmed in cranberry. $175-225.

A German perfume bottle, c.1930s. This small, 3"l, perfume bottle was made to be worn around a woman's neck. It is marked Germany. $60-75.

Czechoslovakian Beads, c.1930s. This is a 20" and a 16" strand of very clear cut vaseline beads. $95-125 and $75-95 respectively.

An Art glass vase, maker unknown, c.1890s. This is a very thin and delicate blown, ribbed vase with an opalescent top. It is 5.25"h x 5.5"d. $245-265. *Courtesy of Laura Kelm and Pete Buck.*

Art glass. This small opalescent vase possibly English is 3.5"h x 2.1"d. $125-150. *Courtesy of Laura Kelm and Pete Buck.*

Blue epergnes, maker unknown, c.1890s. These blown epergnes, possibly of English origin, have the same base. The difference is in the tops of the lilies and the applied rigaree. They measure 15"h x 7"b and 15.5"h x 7"b. $185-200 ea. The taller epergne is *courtesy of Laura Kelm and Pete Buck.*

A Victorian vase, maker unknown, c.1890s. This blown vase, sometimes called a spittoon, has a touch of blue on the top and is 4.25"h. $175-200. *Courtesy of Laura Kelm and Pete Buck.*

Venetian glass vase, c.1880s. This mold blown vase with fluted, opalescent top and clear base is very thin and delicate, 6"h x 3.85"d. $125-150.

Vaseline grapes, maker and circa unknown. This fruit arrangement with a 7"l cluster of vaseline grapes in the center was reported as being bought in an antiquarian shop in France in the 1930s. A string tag on the arrangement read *Fabric Aux Bohem.* $300-350. *Courtesy of Josie Middleton.*

An English condiment set, c.1890s. This is a 5" opalescent bowl with a fluted top and applied rigaree around center, maker unknown. The stand is marked "RSP Co. EPNS" and is 7.5"h x 4.75"sq. The spoon has an ivory handle and is marked EPNS. $225-275.

Epergne. This very delicate canary opalescent glass is possibly of English origin, c.1890s. The men from whom I purchased this piece used it as a table centerpiece for flower arrangements in their home and called it a jardiniere instead of an epergne. The stand is marked E. M. and Co. S. 11.5"h x 12.25"d. $900-950.

Glossary

Acid-Etching. A method using hydrofluoric acid to decorate glass. The acid eats away exposed surfaces thus forming a design in the glass. It resembles engraving but is flatter.

Air Bubbles. Flaws that occur in a piece of glassware when the glass is being formed by the mixture of various chemicals. Many manufacturers have used the bubbles as a way of creating a new design, and may have deliberately placed bubbles inside a glass design.

Annealing. The process of letting the glass gradually cool so that it is stronger than it might normally be if there were rapid cooling. It is a process performed in a special kiln which allows the glass to slowly reach room temperature.

Applied Glass. A separate gather of glass attached to the main gather during blowing and shaping or immediately after pressing.

Blown Glass. Refers to a type of glass made by the process of blowing air into a pipe attached to molten glass. The glass can be blown by mouth or machine into a mold or formed "freehand."

Cased Glass. Glassware that is covered with one or more layers of colored glass. It can be made by blowing the inner layer into each succeeding outer layer while hot or dipping the gather into molten glass of another color.

Cutting. There are two basics ways in which glass is cut. Smoothing the edge or rim of the glass by melting is the hot method. Smoothing the edge or rim of the glass through a sanding process is the cold method. The cutting method is also used to decorate glass by machine or hand.

Decorating. Cold glass can be decorated by: acid washing, cutting, engraving, etching, frosting, and painting. Some techniques for decorating hot glass include: applied relief, crackling, design transfer, lacing, molding, overlaying, pressing, and ribbing.

Engraving. A method using a rapidly rotating stone or copper wheel and an abrasive mixture to decorate glass. The abrasions are shallower than with cutting and have more detail.

Iridescent Finish. A rainbow-like colored finish sprayed on while the glass is warm. This finish is found on carnival glass and art glass.

Lacy-Pattern Glass. Pressed glass characterized by a stippled background and a complex scroll-and-flower design. It was produced from the mid-1820s to mid-1840s.

Mold. A two, three, or four-piece metal or wooden holder used to shape molten glass.

Mold-Marks. When looking at molded glassware, one may be able to see seams in the glass left by the process of shaping the glass and not removed by the manufacturer.

Nappy. A 19th-century term used by manufacturers to describe small bowls of various shapes.

Opalescent Glass. Glass having a bluish-white, translucent color resembling an opal. When held to a very strong light it will show red highlights.

Pressed Glass. Molten glass pressed into a mold that provides the finished shape and pattern is referred to as pressed glass.

Rigaree. A piece of glass applied to an object for decoration.

Salver. A term used in the 18th and 19th centuries to describe a tray or platter on a high stem. This piece could be used for desserts, tea sandwiches, or visiting cards.

Bibliography

Boyd's Crystal Art Glass. *Boyd's Crystal Art Glass, The Tradition Continues.* Cambridge, Ohio.

Bredehoft, Neila and Tom. *Hobbs, Brockunier and Co. Glass.* Paducah, Kentucky: Collector Books, 1997.

Edwards, Bill. *Standard Encyclopedia of Opalescent Glass.* Paducah, Kentucky: Collector Books, 1995.

Florence, Gene. *Degenhart Glass and Paperweights.* Cambridge, Ohio: Degenhart Paperweight and Glass Museum, Inc., 1982.

Glickman, Jay T. *Yellow-Green Vaseline! A Guide to the Magic Glass.* Marietta, Ohio: Antique Publications, 1991.

Heacock, William. *Book II Opalescent Glass from A to Z.* Marietta, Ohio: Antique Publications, 1977.

Heacock, William. *Collecting Glass.* Marietta, Ohio: Antique Publications, 1984.

Heacock, William. *Encyclopedia of Victorian Colored Pattern Glass Book 1 Toothpick Holders from A to Z.* Marietta, Ohio: Antique Publications, 2nd edition, 1976.

Heacock, William. *Fenton Glass, The First Twenty-Five Years.* Marietta, Ohio: O-Val Advertising Corp., 1978.

Heacock, William. *Fenton Glass, The Second Twenty-Five Years.* Marietta, Ohio: O-Val Advertising Corp., 1980.

Heacock, William. *Fenton Glass, The Third Twenty-Five Years.* Marietta, Ohio: O-Val Advertising Corp., 1989.

Heacock, William. *The Glass Collector.* Marietta, Ohio: Peacock Publications, 1983.

Heacock, William. *1000 Toothpick Holders.* Marietta, Ohio: Antique Publications, 1977.

Heacock, William. *Rare and Unlisted Toothpick Holders.* Marietta, Ohio: Antique Publications, 1984.

Heacock, William. *Victorian Colored Pattern Glass Book III.* Marietta, Ohio: Antique Publications, 1976.

Heacock, William. *Victorian Colored Pattern Glass Book 6 Oil Cruets From A to Z.* Marietta, Ohio: Antique Publications, 1981.

Heacock, William, and Bickenhauser, Fred. *Victorian Colored Pattern Glass Book 5 U.S. Glass from A to Z.* Marietta, Ohio: Antique Publications, 1978.

Heacock, William, and Johnson, Patricia. *5,000 Open Salts, A Collector's Guide.* Marietta, Ohio: Antique Publications, 1995.

Heacock, William; Measell, James; Wiggins, Berry. *Dugan/Diamond The Story of Indiana, Pennsylvania, Glass.* Marietta, Ohio: Antique Publications, 1993.

Heacock, William; Measell, James; Wiggins, Berry. *Harry Northwood The Early Years 1881-1900.* Marietta, Ohio: Antique Publications, 1990.

Intercon Arts. *Glass.* Miami, Florida: Intercon Arts, 1984.

Jenks, Bill, and Luna, Jerry. *Early American Pattern Glass 1850-1910.* Radnor, Pennsylvania: Wallace-Homestead Book Company, 1990.

Jenks, Bill; Luna, Jerry; and Reilly, Darryl. *Identifying Pattern Glass Reproductions.* Radnor, Pennsylvania: Wallace-Homestead, 1993.

McCain, Mollie Helen. *The Collector's Encyclopedia of Pattern Glass.* Paducah, Kentucky: Collector Books, 1982.

McKearin, George S. and Helen. *American Glass.* Bonanza Books, New York, New York, 1989.

Measell, James. *Fenton Glass, The 1980s Decade.* Marietta, Ohio: Antique Publications, 1996.

Measell, James. *Imperial Glass Encyclopedia Volume II.* Marietta, Ohio: Antique Publications, 1997.

Measell, James, and Roetteis, W.C. "Red". *The L.G. Wright Glass Company.* Marietta, Ohio: Antique Publications, 1997.

National Cambridge Collectors, Inc. *The Cambridge Glass Co.* Paducah, Kentucky: Collector Books, 1991.

Phillips, Phoebe. *Encyclopedia of Glass.* Great Britain: Octopus Books Limited, 1981.

Pina, Leslie. *Fifties Glass.* Atglen, Pennsylvania: Schiffer Publishing Ltd., 1997.

Revi, Albert Christian. *Nineteenth Century Glass.* New York: Galahad Books, 1967.

Richardson, David E. *Glass Collector's Digest.* Marietta, Ohio: The Glass Press, Inc., 1997.

Thuro, Catherine M.V. *Oil Lamps, The Kerosene Era in North America.* Radnor, Pennsylvania: Wallace-Homestead, 1992.

Thuro, Catherine M.V. *Oil Lamps II, Glass Kerosene Lamps.* Paducah, Kentucky: Collector's Books, 1992.

Webber, Norman W. *Collecting Glass.* New York: Arco Publishing Company, 1978.

Whitmyer, Margaret and Kenn. *Bedroom and Bathroom Glassware.* Paducah, Kentucky: Collector Books, 1990.

Whitmyer, Margaret and Kenn. *Fenton Art Glass.* Paducah, Kentucky: Collector Books, 1996.

Yalom, Libby. *Shoes of Glass.* Marietta, Ohio: Antique Publications, 1988.

Index